Advance Praise for

Believe!

"When so many despair at America's future, we need a reminder of who we are and why the best lies ahead. The re-release of Rich DeVos' classic *Believe!* couldn't come at a better time. Read this book and your optimism will rise."

—**Arthur C. Brooks**, Harvard Professor and
#1 *New York Times* bestselling author

"*Believe!* reminds us that the strength of a country lies in the strength of its people and in the principles they choose to live by."

—**Charles Koch**, CEO of Koch Industries
and *New York Times* bestselling author

"Rich and Doug DeVos—father and son—offer a powerful reminder of the timeless principles that shape strong families and a free society. As we look to what's possible in our country today, these lessons are as important as they've ever been."

—**Chase Koch**, Executive Vice President of Koch Industries

"There's no better occasion than America's 250th anniversary to reaffirm our commitment to these core principles. Rich DeVos and *Believe!* exemplify the best of America—including optimism, positivity, and commitment to principles of the Declaration of Independence and the Constitution."

—**Jeffery Rosen**, President and CEO of
National Constitution Center

"My dad, evangelist Luis Palau, was great friends with Rich DeVos for almost fifty years. They shared a love for America—Dad's adopted country. And they shared the conviction that loving God and loving people is what makes life worth living. The principles shared in *Believe!* are just as timely today as they were fifty years ago. And practicing them can bring the personal and national renewal we all long for!"

—**Kevin Palau**, President and CEO of Palau

"Rich DeVos was one of those rare individuals who used words the way a master artist uses paint—carefully, purposefully, and always in service of creating something meaningful. His language wasn't just communication—it was the palette for a life's masterpiece."

—**Jim Hackett**, Former President and CEO of Ford Motor Company

Believe!

Believe!

A Timeless Endorsement
of American Principles

Rich DeVos

With New Reflections by Doug DeVos

Post Hill
PRESS

Post Hill Press
New York • Nashville
posthillpress.com

Published in the United States of America
1 2 3 4 5 6 7 8 9 10

To my wife, Helen, and our children Dick, Dan, Cheri, Doug,
whom I love very much.

—**Rich DeVos**, 1975

On behalf of my siblings, all of our children, grandchildren,
and future generations. We still believe!

—**Doug DeVos**, 2025

Acknowledgments

Special thanks to Charles Paul Conn for his invaluable contribution to the original text of *Believe!*. His skillful storytelling and thoughtful collaboration helped bring my father's vision and message to life, leaving a lasting impact on readers for generations.

A heartfelt acknowledgment to the late Billy Zeoli, a lifelong friend and spiritual counselor to my father, with whom he spent a great deal of time and energy sharing these principles with audiences around the world.

—Doug DeVos

Table of Contents

Foreword

By Steve Van Andel

Believing is the first step toward leading a more optimistic and fulfilling life.

When Doug shared with me his idea to reissue his dad's book and update it with thoughts of his own, I knew it would be great—and that the timing couldn't be better. Similar to when *Believe!* was first published, the world is once again feeling complicated, unpredictable, and a little disconnected. However, it doesn't have to feel that way. What you'll read on the following pages will help to restore what I've found to be the best comfort in times of uncertainty: hope and its close cousin, optimism.

My dad, Jay, met Doug's dad, Rich, in high school and they became the best of friends. After trying their hand at a variety of businesses and having countless adventures together, Dad and Rich settled in Ada, Michigan buying homes right next door to each other. They started what would become the most successful direct selling company in the world: Amway. What drove that success? Their adherence to their values, and their unwavering belief in the amazing ability of people. My dad would say he'd stake the future of the business on it—and they did.

Dad and Rich lived their lives by a strong set of principles that anchored how they saw the world and guided all their actions. These principles were in their DNA. They talked about them at the dinner table. They practiced them in their church and community. They were at the core of everything they did in life and in business.

My dad was the smartest man I've ever known. His sense of optimism was unparalleled, second only to Rich. Rich was a charismatic motivator who could light up a crowd with his words; Dad was a brilliant intellectual who kept the trains running on time. They balanced one another perfectly.

I was about five years old when Dad and Rich started Amway in the basement. As I got older and the company continued to grow, I saw people who started with almost nothing build successful businesses. I saw people find a sense of community and family that they hadn't felt before, and I saw people of all backgrounds and beliefs find greater meaning in their lives. Not just by way of material success, but from the deeper fulfillment that comes from realizing your own potential while also making a difference in the lives of others.

Dad and Rich's partnership was built on a deep and abiding trust in one another. Our dads could enjoy that trust because they lived by the same set of principles and values, just as Doug and I do. We grew up together, going between our two houses, eating dinner together, taking vacations as one big family; it was almost like having two sets of parents with eight kids. We learned by our parents' example how to lead good and honest lives, how to see the best in people, how to trust in each other, and how to believe in ourselves and in a brighter future. These are the same lessons you'll learn about in the pages that follow.

I've got a couple of years on Doug and was already working at Amway when I first saw him speak to a crowd of distributors. He was fresh out of college when he took the stage at a rally held at the Civic Auditorium in downtown Grand Rapids. I knew from that moment, that he had the same magic as his dad to lift people up, encourage them to pursue their dreams, and to believe in the potential of everyone to do good in the world. I knew that the business needed that magic then, and I know that the world needs it now.

Foreword

Doug and I have held a variety of roles at Amway throughout our careers; the most meaningful to me have been the last twenty-five years that I've spent serving alongside him, first as co-chief executives and now as co-chairmen of the board. I couldn't ask for a better business partner or friend.

Doug has done the world a service by offering new thoughts on his dad's time-tested book. (Rich did the world an even greater service by writing the original!) These principles are as powerful today as they were fifty years ago, and I've seen them do incredible things in people's lives. I know they can do the same for you. They will help you make tomorrow better than today.

You'll read in this book that greatness lies within each and every one of us and you will learn how to unlock it within yourself and see it in those around you. Read this book, and then go out there and find out what's possible. As my dad would say, the future is almost always more remarkable than you can imagine... and it starts now. Believe it!

—Steve Van Andel

Introduction

By Doug DeVos

Is America on the verge of an incredible comeback? Or is America in decline?

You've no doubt heard—or maybe asked—one or both questions as our country prepares for its 250th birthday: July 4, 2026, the anniversary of the Declaration of Independence. The 250th anniversary of the Constitution is also just around the corner. As these milestones approach, more and more people want the country to get on a better track.

For the first time in recorded history, fewer than half of Americans think our best days are ahead of us. More people think that our best days are in the rearview mirror.[1]

Four out of five Americans now believe their children's lives will be worse than theirs. That number has doubled in just twenty years.[2]

And when it comes to the long run, more Americans worry that someone born in the future will be worse off than someone born in the past.[3]

But is it true? Is America really in decline?

---

1 https://www.foxnews.com/official-polls/fox-news-poll-americas-best-days-thing-past-voters-think

2 https://www.wsj.com/articles/most-americans-doubt-their-children-will-be-better-off-wsj-norc-poll-finds-35500ba8

3 https://www.thecgo.org/research/abundance-poll/

Introduction

I've asked myself this question, too. And my answer is resounding: No!

I don't think we're declining.

I think we're *drifting*.

There's a big difference. We're lost at sea—wondering who we are and where we're going. We don't feel anchored to the core ideas that created the American experiment and the American Dream. Instead, we're distracted by the latest idea or shiny object. When you're drifting, you get taken by the current or blown by the wind, rudderless.

Sure enough, America isn't moving in a clear direction, which usually means we're going in the wrong direction. As someone who likes to sail, I know how dangerous this is. Even if you're just a couple of degrees off course, after a while, you'll end up nowhere near where you want to be—where you *should* be.

America remains the strongest country on Earth by a variety of measures, with plenty of advantages. But we're not moving intentionally or strongly to where we need to go and what we need to be.

And we're not the only ones who need America to do better. I often find myself in other countries and cultures. The discussion usually turns to the USA and what's happening here. America sets the tone. The world needs us to find our bearings, nearly as much as we need to find it for our own sake.

But America is still in a position to lead—and that's good news! We just need to remember who we are and what we stand for, and build a future on the ideals that made us great in the first place. And the solution starts with…

You.

Our future—*your* future—is a self-fulfilling prophecy. If you believe that tomorrow is going to be worse, you'll act accordingly. You'll strive less and try less. You'll try to get more than you give because, after all, things are bad, so who cares?

Believe!

But if you believe that tomorrow will be better, you'll act very differently.

Instead of sitting back, you'll step up. Instead of accepting the problems around us, you'll ask how you can solve them. You'll never settle for the *status quo*—because you know you can chart a brighter future.

Ultimately, you'll make the most of your own life, achieving more than you imagine. And in the process, you'll show your community and our country what's possible.

If you don't do it, who will?

My dad posed that question all the time. Years ago, he spoke at a college graduation. The economy was in rough shape and the graduates were worried about whether they'd succeed. But Dad told them to ignore everyone who was focused on the bad times. He told those graduates: "It doesn't matter if it's a good time or a bad time; now is the only time you got."

What was true then is true now. The book you hold in your hands is built on that belief—in the faith in your ability to make an incredible difference and achieve extraordinary things.

Dad first wrote this book fifty years ago. It was the 1970s. Then, like now, it looked like America was drifting. Dad wanted to help people rediscover our national rudder, steering themselves and society in the right direction.

What is that rudder? *Time-tested principles.*

With the right principles that have been proven to work, we can move purposefully in the right direction. If we want America to stop drifting, we need to remember those principles—as individuals and then as a country.

Those time-tested principles are what Dad talked about, wrote about, and lived out his entire life. They're the core of this book. Each one gets its own chapter. Dad and his best friend, Jay Van Andel, built their business, Amway, around them. The company's name is short for "American Way," and for Dad and Jay, these principles are the American Way. They enable people to realize their incredible potential, achieve seemingly unimaginable dreams, and transform their communities and country through everyday actions by everyday people.

Now, I know what you're thinking: This book was written a long time ago. Maybe you weren't even born! (I was eleven, for the record.) There's been so much change in the past fifty years; surely this book must be woefully out of date, especially since I've kept all the original text my dad wrote.

Sure, some of his language reflects the 1970s. The Soviet Union, anyone? So, I've given some new thoughts and stories at the start of each chapter. Some are from my experiences and some are from my dad's life after he wrote this book—he lived another forty-two years. Hopefully, these stories connect each principle to the challenges and opportunities of today. You'll also find some tips on how to practice these principles. It looks different for everyone.

But overall, you'll find that most of this book has aged exceptionally well. No wonder: These principles aren't tethered to any particular era. They're unchanging truths that can help you navigate changing times—a true rudder.

Dad's story is proof. In 1975, Amway was barely fifteen years old, but these principles had already demonstrated their power through the people who started their own Amway businesses. Thousands of people across this country, and increasingly around the world, were achieving their goals and creating a better future for themselves and their families. Fifty years later, millions of people have now done this through Amway.

But the American Way has never been just about business. These same principles play a role in everything our family did and other businesses in which we've become involved. We use them with sports teams, including the NBA's Orlando Magic. And these principles are part of the DNA of our entire family. Me, my wife and our kids, my siblings, and their families, too.

Believe!

Most importantly, these principles are being applied daily by people around the world, from every walk of life. They prove that the American Way is equally powerful in other countries and cultures. These principles are just as essential to the future of everyone in South America, Europe, Asia, and Africa—indeed, to everyone in the world.

My personal experience is tied to our businesses, our community, and our country.

Consider the story of Grand Rapids. A year after this book was first published, President Gerald Ford came to his (and our) hometown after losing the 1976 presidential campaign. Despite his loss, the city wanted to throw its favorite son a parade on the main street of downtown. However, the Secret Service wouldn't allow it because hardly any buildings on the route were occupied.

Talk about embarrassing. Our favorite son, the president of the United States, was here, and we couldn't honor and celebrate him the way we wanted to. Our city's failure was a wake-up call.

And so we woke up. Collectively, we looked at ourselves and recognized that we were not the city we wanted to be or needed to be for future generations. So we went back to the foundations of what made our city good in the first place and began to turn things around. I was still quite young at the time, but I had a front-row seat to the transformation that followed.

My dad really kicked things off by investing his time, talent, and treasure to make things better, beginning downtown. He led the charge for a new convention center that anchored the area's renaissance. And what he started, others continued—founding new businesses, building hotels, expanding hospitals, strengthening universities, and driving innovation and energy at every turn.

It wasn't just one big thing. It was a few big things, some medium-sized things, and lots and lots of small things that added up quickly. It felt like everyone in Grand Rapids was part of it, and as I got older, I got involved, too. Together, we did the seemingly impossible!

Introduction

Today's Grand Rapids is a far cry from what it was fifty years ago because a lot of people decided to do something about it. We're one of the fastest-growing cities in the country, a wonderful place to visit, and a great place to raise a family. Sure, we still have problems to solve and work to do. We can always be better and we have to provide more opportunities for everyone in our community. But we know we can get there—if we all get together and make it happen ourselves.

That's the kind of upward-looking, forward-moving, problem-solving attitude America needs right now. Not in some abstract or academic sense. We all need to make this practical and personal, applying time-tested principles to make a difference in ways that no one else can.

Here's the bottom line: You can't wait for someone else to save America. Not politicians, as important as they are. Not business or community leaders, either. The real leaders in this country are you and me and all our fellow citizens. And while that may seem daunting, it's empowering, too. The future depends on you. You're more important than you ever knew!

Dad understood this. While he may have written this book fifty years ago, the seeds of his wisdom were planted in his childhood.

He grew up in a faith-filled Christian family and community. He knew he was a child of God and he lived his life with that understanding. Their family struggled through the Great Depression of the 1930s and went from there right into World War Two. Amid all the challenges, his father continued to encourage him and reminded him that they weren't stuck—that the future was going to be bright. All they had to do was believe and work hard to get through the trials of the day.

Dad did just that. He and Jay both served in the war, and they wrote letters to each other to stay in touch. They complained to each other a bit, but they also encouraged each other a lot. They wrote about what they wanted to do with their lives: "Someday this war is going to end. Someday we'll be back home. Someday we'll get into business together."

They knew that our country's existence was at stake. They knew their way of life hung in the balance. But they also knew that they had a duty to make a difference. When they returned, like so many others, they went to work. They made the most of every single opportunity that came their way because they'd faced the fear that there may not be a future. That's how they made the future so much better—for themselves and so many others.

Fast forward to our time. We're not in the middle of a global war, though the world isn't exactly peaceful. But we are in the midst of a struggle for our future.

As the principles in this book have fallen out of favor or been forgotten, they've been replaced—and not for the better. We'll explore some of these competing ideas at the start of each chapter, but for now, let's just say that I believe the answers are right in front of us.

And if we don't start building our future on these principles, America's drift may indeed become a decline.

Given the stakes, this book is even more timely than it was in 1975. These principles can help you make the most of your life. They can help you build a strong family, an incredible career, and a vibrant community. And they can help us all build a society that empowers people to achieve their own American Dream—everyone, without exception.

Can we do it? Of course we can! We aren't stuck. We have everything we need to move forward because we have you.

Our people are still the most creative and entrepreneurial on Earth. Our economy is still the envy of the world. Hundreds of millions of people want to live in the land of the free and the home of the brave. And our country's history is one of incredible progress, driven by everyday people.

The promise of America has always been a brighter future, and for 250 years, Americans have worked hard to make that future brighter. We've overcome evils like slavery, ended restrictions on women's rights, and given more and more people a real opportunity to live their best life. We've worked to make our union a bit more perfect with every generation. We're not there yet and we still have a lot of work to do together. Yet in our hearts, we know it can be done, and you're essential!

Dad showed me and thousands upon thousands of others what's possible. I saw him live the principles in this book every day. They didn't just help him succeed in business. They helped him be an incredible father to me and my siblings, an incredible husband to my mother, and an incredible servant in his church and community. I miss him every day, but I'm glad he gave me the lasting gift of his example. He proved that these principles are key to a good life.

Now it's our turn to prove it. It's your turn.

May this book inspire you to embrace the opportunities that can transform your future, your community, and our nation. May you find extraordinary success and then reach out to help others succeed too.

And may you prove—to yourself and to others—that America's days of drifting are over. As long as you stand by and live by these principles, our country's future is bright indeed!

—*Doug DeVos*

Believe!

...in Unlimited Potential

Introduction

What's at the heart of the American experiment? It's not merely freedom or liberty. It's not our system of checks and balances. What makes America truly exceptional is that we were the first country to recognize something universal and profound. America is built on a deep belief in people—a belief that everyone's someone—that *you're* exceptional.

This truth is clear from the beginning of our country—from some of the first words of our Declaration of Independence. We're all "created equal." We all have "unalienable rights." And that includes the rights of "Life, Liberty, and the pursuit of Happiness."

No doubt, America has fallen short of practicing this belief in people. Thankfully, Americans have earnestly strived to right our wrongs, and our greatest successes have come from empowering those who've been oppressed or overlooked. To this day, we continue to give more and more folks the chance to make the most of their lives, breaking the many barriers that stand in their way. America remains the envy of the world precisely because we believe in empowering everyone to make the most of their life.

But in recent years, we've lost some of that belief in people—that belief in *you*. The results aren't pretty.

Consider what's known as "deaths of despair." Deaths from suicide, drug addiction, and alcohol abuse are soaring. Maybe you

1

know someone who's gone down that dark road. Maybe it was a friend or, God forbid, a family member. It's heartbreaking.

It's also what happens when we stop believing in each other. A growing number of Americans no longer think other folks are worth much. Maybe they hold the "wrong" views, live in the "wrong" place, or act the "wrong" way.

Once you start down that mental road, it's easy to justify ignoring them, treating them like garbage, and even denying them their rights. Rights like free speech, equal opportunity, and equal treatment under the law. Sound familiar? These are your rights—your birthright—and they're in danger.

But the damage doesn't end there. When other people don't believe in you, it's easy to stop believing in yourself. *Do I really have something to offer society? Am I capable of making a difference in my community? Maybe they're right—I'm actually worthless.* But nothing could be further from the truth!

As a country, we have to rediscover our belief in people—our belief in you. All of us have incredible gifts, including you. All of us have an even more incredible capacity to grow and contribute, including you. Recognizing this fact is truly empowering. You *are* worth something. You *can* make a difference. You *will* pursue your potential with every fiber of your being. And you *will* think the same way about others—because you believe in them, too.

Imagine if every American thought that way. Imagine if every American *acted* that way. Our national and individual malaise would begin to fade, replaced by the dogged pursuit of a brighter future for all.

A few years after Dad wrote *Believe!*, I joined him on a trip to Malaysia while I was in high school. While we were there, Dad had an experience that he shared countless times—a story I repeat as often as possible.

Amway had been in Malaysia for a few years, and we were visiting for Amway Malaysia's first National Convention. Thousands of relatively new Amway business owners were coming, and it was quite a significant celebration. It was such a big deal, the Amway team had arranged for Dad to have a meeting with the prime minister of Malaysia.

During their meeting, the prime minister expressed his worries about the Malaysian economy. He said he was concerned that the prices of copper, tin, and oil were depressed on the global market. He called these commodities Malaysia's "greatest national resources" and said low prices were causing a lot of problems. He then changed the subject to Amway's rapid growth, noting the thousands of Amway business owners who were coming to the National Convention. He asked Dad about the secret to Amway's success.

Dad's response was simple and direct. He said, "Mr. Prime Minister, you may believe that Malaysia's greatest natural resources are copper, tin, and oil, but we believe the greatest natural resources of Malaysia are the people of Malaysia, and at Amway, we invest in people!"

That belief in people is true at all times and in all places—including America. Our greatest resource isn't anything we have. It's everyone we have. And to make the most of our future, we need to recognize and unleash everyone's unlimited potential.

At the end of the day, renewing our belief in people—our belief in *you*—is how we'll get started on another 250 years of opportunity and progress. After all, you can do it. And no one can do it better than you.

—Doug DeVos

THOSE PEOPLE WHOSE AIM IS ALWAYS LOW generally hit what they shoot at: they aim for nothing and hit it.

Life need not be lived that way. I believe that one of the most powerful forces in the world is the will of the man who believes in himself, who dares to aim high, to go confidently after the things that he wants from life.

"I can." It is a powerful sentence: I can. It is amazing how many people can use that sentence realistically. For the overwhelming majority of people, that sentence can be a true one. It works. People can do what they believe they can do. Apart from the few people in the world who are deluded in a psychotic sense, the gap between what a man thinks he can achieve and what is actually possible to him is very, very small. But first he must believe that he can.

Let's get one thing straight: I do not pretend to be an expert on the subject of motivation. I have no more knowledge of what motivates men than does the average person. Since Amway has grown so rapidly, and since its success has depended on two hundred thousand self-employed distributors, I am often asked for my notions of motivation. "What makes some people succeed when others fail?" they want to know. Or they ask for my "secrets" on motivation, as if I can deliver some profound bit of wisdom about why one man sets new sales records while another folds up and quits. I hate to disappoint these people, but the simple fact is that I have no gimmicks or tricks or magic words to make people succeed.

But although I cannot claim any special knowledge of motivational techniques, I do have a firm conviction that almost anyone can do whatever he really believes he can do.

The nature of the goal really makes little difference. When I was a young man, I had an ambition to go into business for myself and succeed at it. That was "my thing," as the current expression has it. I was not particularly interested in finishing college, or traveling around the world, or becoming the leading golfer on the PGA tour or the top man in the Michigan legislature. There is nothing wrong with those things—they all are legitimate goals—but they just didn't happen to appeal to me at the time. My goal was to succeed in my own business, and I believed that I could do it.

There is no way ever to know for sure, of course, but I believe the result would have been much the same whatever my goal had been. The point is that there are no areas of life which are immune to the combination of faith and effort. The personal philosophy of "I can" does not apply just to business but to politics, education, church work, athletics, the arts, you name it. It cuts across all lines. It can be the greatest common factor in such diverse accomplishments as earning a Ph.D., making a million dollars, becoming a five-star general, or riding a winner at Churchill Downs.

I look back at the forty-odd years of my life, and it seems that more than any other single lesson, my experiences have conspired to teach me the value of determined, confident effort. For most of my life, I have been associated with Jay Van Andel. We started the Amway company together in 1959, but long before that—since we were teenagers in high school, in fact—we were sharing experiences that taught us forcibly the excitement of "I can."

When World War II ended, Jay and I came home convinced that the aviation business was the hot item of the future. We had visions of airplanes in every garage, millions of people learning to fly, that sort of thing. So we wanted to go into the aviation business. We had a few hundred dollars, bought a little Piper Cub airplane, and got ready to open an aviation school. There was a minor problem: neither of us knew how to fly an airplane!

Believe!

We didn't let that stop us. We simply hired experienced pilots to give the flying lessons while we stayed busy with the work of selling those lessons to the public. The point is that we had decided to operate a flying service, and we refused to let anything dampen our enthusiasm—not even a small detail like not knowing how to fly.

We hit another snag—when we got our customers signed up and our instructors hired, we discovered that the runways at the little airport had not been completed yet. They were still nothing but giant streaks of mud. We improvised. A river ran alongside the airport, so we bought some floats for our Piper Cub and flew right off the water, taking off and landing on those bloated pontoon floats. (We eventually had two students who graduated from our course who had never landed an airplane on dry land!)

We were supposed to have offices there at the little airstrip, but the time came to open our business and the offices were still not built. Something had to be done. A chicken coop was bought from a farmer down the road, hauled over to the airstrip, whitewashed, a padlock put on the door, and a sign hung that read grandly: Wolverine Air Service. We had set out to get into the aviation business and we were in it.

The end of that story is that we built a thriving business, bought a dozen airplanes, and eventually had one of the biggest aviation services in town. But we made it only because from the very start, we believed in ourselves. We felt in our bones that we could do it, and we did, despite those early roadblocks. If we had launched the project half-heartedly, not quite believing in it, always looking over our shoulders for an excuse to lie down and quit, the first plane would never have made the first flight—there never would have been a Wolverine Air Service.

That story illustrates a basic point: one never knows what he might accomplish until he tries. That is so simple that some people completely overlook it. If we had listened to all the logical arguments against our air service in those days, we would never have attempted it. We would have given up before we started, and to this day we would assume that we could not have made a go of it. We would still sit around and talk about that great idea that didn't work. But it did work, because we believed in it and committed ourselves enough to try it.

Also, after that, we decided to try our hands at the restaurant business. Not that we knew anything at all about the restaurant business—we didn't—but we had been out to California and seen drive-in restaurants for the first time. Grand Rapids had nothing like that, we thought, and we believed we could make a drive-in restaurant go in our hometown. So we tried it. We bought a prefabricated building, put a one-man kitchen inside, and were all ready for the grand opening. When opening night came, the power company had not connected the electricity. Temporary panic. But we never once entertained the idea of postponing the opening. We rented a generator at the last minute, set it up in that squatty little building, and cranked out our own electricity. The restaurant opened right on schedule.

That little restaurant never became the biggest money-maker in the world, but it was a going venture. One day, Jay would cook while I hopped cars; the next day, we would reverse roles. (It was a terrible way to try to make a living!) But the important thing is that we put our minds to doing the thing we had set out to do, instead of just sitting around and talking about it. We could have talked about it for years. We could have worried about all the problems and reflected on the obstacles and never gotten around to *doing* it. So we would never have known whether or not we could succeed in the restaurant business.

What does all this say? Give things a chance to happen! Give success a chance to happen! It is impossible to win the race unless you venture to run, impossible to win the victory unless you dare to battle. No life is more tragic than that of the individual who nurses a dream, an ambition, always wishing and hoping, but never giving it a chance to happen. He nurses the flickering dream, but never lets it break out into flame. Millions of people are that way about having a second income, or owning their own business, and Amway is designed somewhat in response to that need. There are millions more who nurture private, almost secret dreams in other areas: the schoolteacher who wants to go back for that master's degree; the small businessman who dreams of expanding his business; the couple who has intended to make that trip to Europe; the housewife whose ambition is to write short stories for the freelance market. The list could go on and on. People dreaming but never daring, never willing to say, "I can," never trusting their dreams to the real world of action and effort—people, in short, who are so afraid of failure that they fail.

For the individual in that position, there is only one thing left after all the arguments are weighed and all the costs measured. Do it. Try it. Quit talking about it and do it. How will you ever know if you can paint that picture, run that business, sell that vacuum cleaner, earn that degree, hold that office, make that speech, win that game, marry that girl, write that book, bake that soufflé, build that house—unless you try it!

My early experiences with Jay were so dominated with this kind of attitude that we did things which, looking back, seem almost foolhardy. But we were so eager to try our hand at new things and so confident that they would come out right that we just floated along on a cloud of "I can." And usually we found that we could! But to know that, first we had to try.

We read a book—before either of us was married—that really turned us on to sailing. The book was written by a fellow who had sailed around the Caribbean, and it was filled with the adventures of the high seas. So we decided to sail to South America. We had worked hard and deserved a break, a vacation. We bought an old thirty-eight-foot schooner in Connecticut and got ready for a big trip. We planned to sail down the eastern coast of the United States to Florida and then over to Cuba, then down through the Caribbean to see all the exotic islands, and eventually wind up in South America. We were going to have a wonderful time. The only problem was that neither of us had ever been on a sailboat in our lives. Never.

I remember going to Holland, Michigan, one day and asking a fellow in a sailboat to give us a ride. "Why should I give you a ride?" he asked.

I said, "Well, we just bought a thirty-eight-footer, and we've never sailed in our lives."

"Where are you planning to go in it?" he asked. And when we told him South America, he almost passed out right on the dock.

But we believed we could.

We picked up our boat, got a few quick lessons, and set sail with the book in one hand and the tiller in the other. We got lost immediately. We got lost so badly in New Jersey that even the Coast Guard couldn't find us. We missed two turns at night and got way back up in the inland marshes someplace. When the Coast Guard finally found us after an all-day search, they couldn't believe where we were. "Nobody has ever been this far inland in a boat this size before," they declared and hauled us unceremoniously back out to the ocean with a rope.

That was a wonderful old boat, except for a habit it developed of leaking, which might be considered a rather bad habit for a boat. We finally got to Florida, pumping water out of the bottom of that boat all the way. We would set the alarm for three o'clock every morning to get up and put the pump on, or by five o'clock we would practically be bailing water out by hand. By the time we got to Havana, the situation improved and we hoped our troubles were over. We turned down the northern coast of Cuba, and one dark night the old schooner just gave up and began to sink in 1,500 feet of water, ten miles off the coast. The first ship that came in sight was a big Dutch ship—which would have made a beautiful ending to the story, since Jay and I are both of Dutch ancestry, except this Dutch ship wouldn't pick us up. The men on board just radioed and reported that they had spotted a crummy old Cuban boat in distress and went on their way. An hour later an American ship from New Orleans picked us up and deposited us in Puerto Rico.

Did we give up then and go home?

We didn't even consider it. We had arrived in Puerto Rico in a fashion different from our plans, to be sure, but we were there nevertheless. Back home in Michigan, our folks thought, "Oh well, now those two young boys will be coming home." The thought never occurred to us. We notified our insurance company, told them where to send the money, and kept right on traveling. We went all through the Caribbean, through the major countries of South America, and eventually returned to Michigan right on schedule.

That trip was not a matter of life-or-death importance; it wasn't as significant as a career or a family; it was just a trip, a lark, a time for two young guys to get out and see a little piece of the world. But it came at a meaningful time for me, because it reinforced this growing conviction that the only thing that stands between a man and what he wants from life is often merely the will to try it and the faith to believe that it is possible. After thirty years in business, nothing I have learned has weakened that conviction.

Why do so many people let their dreams die unlived? The biggest reason, I suppose, is the negative, cynical attitudes of other people. Those other people are not enemies—they are friends, even family members. Our enemies never bother us greatly; we can usually handle them with little trouble. But our friends—if they are naysayers, constantly punching holes in our dreams with a cynical smile here, a put-down there, a constant stream of negative vibrations—our friends can kill us! A man gets excited about the possibility of a new job. He sees the opportunity to make more money, do more meaningful work, rise to a personal challenge; the old heart starts pounding and the juices begin to flow and he feels himself revving up for this stimulating new prospect. But then he tells his neighbor about it over the back fence one evening. He gets a smirk, a laugh, that says, "You can't do that," a foot-long list of all the problems and obstacles, and fifty reasons why he never will make it and is better off to stay where he is.

Before he knows it, his enthusiasm falls down to near zero. He goes back into the house like a whipped pup with his tail dragging the ground and all the fire and self-confidence is gone and he begins to second-guess himself. Now he is thinking of all the reasons that he *can't* make it instead of the reasons that he can. He lets one five-minute spiel of negativism or ridicule or just plain disbelief from a dream-nothing, do-nothing neighbor take the steam right out of his engine. Friends like that can do more damage than a dozen enemies.

A young housewife decides to take knitting lessons so she can knit sweaters, afghans, all sorts of things. She gets a book and the needles and yarn and starts to learn the simplest knitting steps, full of visions of brightly colored mittens and clothes. Then her husband comes home from work and tells her how hard it is to knit, how she'll have to work years to be any good at it, how many women have started and quit. He gives her one of those patented, patronizing smiles that says, "You'll never learn to knit very well, you poor thing." And before he has left the room she is believing more in his cynicism than in her faith.

Remember that the easiest thing to find on God's green Earth is someone to tell you all the things you cannot do. Someone will always be eager to point out to you—perhaps merely with a look or a tone of voice—that anything new or daring which you try is hopelessly doomed to failure. Don't listen to them! It is always the fellow who has never made ten thousand dollars a year who knows all the reasons why you can't make fifteen thousand. In the Boy Scouts, it is always the tenderfoot who can recite the reasons that you can't make Eagle Scout. It is the college flunk-out who can explain why you are too dumb to get that degree; the fellow who never ran a business who can best describe the obstacles that make it impossible to get started; the girl who never entered a golf tournament who can most convincingly tell you why you don't have a chance to win. Don't listen to them! If you have a dream, whatever it is, dare to believe it and to try it. Give it a chance to happen! Don't let your brother-in-law or your plumber or your husband's fishing buddy or the guy in the next office rob you of that faith in yourself that makes things happen. Don't let the guys who lie on the couch and watch television every night tell you how futile life is. If you have that flame of a dream down inside you somewhere, thank God for it, and do something about it. And don't let anyone else blow it out.

My father was a great believer in the potential of individual effort. Every time he heard me say the word "can't" as a boy, he would say, "There is no such word as 'can't,' and if you say it one more time I'll knock your block right through that wall!" He never did that, but I never forgot the point he was making. I learned that there really are no good uses of the word "can't."

Believe you can, and you'll find that you can! Try! You'll be surprised at how many good things can happen.

Believe!

...in Accountability

Introduction

One of the most amazing things in America today is happening somewhere you'd never expect.

In a boxing gym. In downtown Detroit. And it's filled with kids. Kids who are transforming their lives—and taking charge of their futures.

Downtown Boxing Gym is unlike anything I've ever seen. It was started by Khali Sweeney, a high-school dropout who couldn't read or write. But he knew how to run the streets of Detroit by the age of eighteen.

One day, a family member showed Khali a picture of him and his friends when they were kids. He told Khali they were all dead—shot on the same streets Khali was running. He asked Khali if that's how he wanted to end up, too.

Khali realized he didn't want to die or end up in jail. The next day, he started to teach himself to read. Then he devoted his life to helping kids in Detroit to transform their lives through education, too.

That's the mission of Downtown Boxing Gym. It doesn't start with books. It starts with boxing. Once the kids are hooked, the books come next.

Khali does something these kids have never experienced. He sets expectations for them. And he demands that the kids meet those expectations. Lo and behold, they do. In a city where you're expected to drop out of high school, 100 percent of the kids at Downtown Boxing Gym graduate.

What Khali is doing is truly countercultural. Today, a lot of people choose victimhood over accountability. When was the last time you heard someone talk about expectations? The very word is usually viewed as something to be avoided at all costs. *Don't impose your expectations on me! I shouldn't even impose them on myself! I'm a victim!*

But expectations aren't an imposition. Expectations are fundamentally empowering.

When you set expectations for yourself, you're saying: *I believe in myself.* And when others set expectations for you, it says: *They believe in me, too. I can rise to the occasion. I can meet—and even exceed—a high bar. I'm capable of so much more than I realize!*

Expectations can't be separated from the principle of accountability. When we hold ourselves and others accountable, we're judging actions against a standard. Standards are good. In fact, without standards, we'll never be great.

Accountability cuts both ways. It means being called out for not hitting the mark as well as being celebrated for your achievement. When expectations are clear, you have a target to focus on. But when expectations aren't clear or don't exist, you're aimless, rudderless. You start drifting and making excuses.

"How was I supposed to figure it out?"

"I wasn't treated fairly."

"It's someone else's fault."

Doesn't that describe what we're feeling in America today? It seems like hardly anyone is willing to take responsibility for their own actions, much less apply their abilities to the fullest extent.

That's what this is really about: making the most of the gifts you've been given. Success doesn't come by sitting still and hoping for the best. Success comes from setting goals and striving to meet them. Accountability is key to getting there. As my friend Ian Rowe put it in a recent book, accountability and personal agency can help overcome the victimhood mentality that holds people back.

I have seen the power of accountability and agency firsthand. Early in my career at Amway, I was given an opportunity to move to Europe for an assignment. Honestly, I wasn't sure I wanted it. I worried I wasn't prepared, that I might fail. I had lots of good reasons (excuses!) why I didn't think I should go. But my wife thought it would be great and was practically packing right after I told her about the possibility! We decided to accept the assignment despite my reservations.

A few weeks before it was time to leave, Jay Van Andel—Amway's cofounder, along with my dad—invited me to his office. He talked about the opportunity ahead of me, giving me lots of advice and encouragement. Then he said something I'll never forget. He said, "Doug, I'm really counting on you to do a great job over there."

I froze. *Really? Are you sure? Don't you know how scared I am and that I really don't want to go? I'm too young and inexperienced. I'm not sure I know what I'm doing. And you're counting on* me?

Jay wasn't one to accept excuses and he expected people to do great things. That's the essence of accountability. He set the standard for me and expected me to rise to the occasion. After that meeting, I realized that if I wanted to succeed, I had to turn his belief in me into personal behavior. In the end, I met his expectations. And to this day, I reflect on Jay's words whenever I face situations that are challenging.

What do people expect of you? What do you expect of yourself? Your beliefs have to become personal behaviors. And as Americans, we can set the bar higher and then work together to reach it, through our own personal agency. When we do, we'll stop celebrating mediocrity, excusing failure, or embracing victimhood. Instead, we'll pursue excellence. Just like the kids who are transforming their lives at the Downtown Boxing Gym.

—*Doug DeVos*

THE CONCEPT OF ACCOUNTABILITY goes all the way back to the Garden of Eden; it is as old as man himself. Adam and Eve tasted the apple and, before the day was over, were held accountable for what they had done. After trying to finesse the issue with the fig leaves and all that, they accepted responsibility for what they had done and were driven from the garden.

Just as we can trace the concept of accountability back to Adam and Eve, we need go only to Cain and Abel to find an example of someone trying to escape accountability for his behavior. Cain killed Abel, then gave the world its first lesson in passing the buck.

When Jehovah called on Cain for a reckoning for Abel's death, the murdering brother countered with a response that still stands as a classic example of the evasive nonanswer: "Am I my brother's keeper?" (Genesis 4:9)

The answer, of course, was yes. Yes, Cain was accountable. Just as Adam and Eve were accountable. Just as you and I are accountable. Accountability—the demand that each individual takes full responsibility for his choices and actions, the willingness to accept the rewards or punishment that follow as natural consequences of his behavior. Accountability is the glue that holds a society together. It is the common agreement by the members of any society that they will be responsible in their dealings with one another. Accountability is having to answer to someone for what one does.

Everyone is accountable to someone—or should be. The employees of a manufacturing company draw their per-hour wages at the end of the week, and consequently are accountable to their foreman for how they spend time on the job during that week. The foreman, on the other hand, is accountable to the supervisor, and he to the manager, and so forth, to the chief executive officer of the company for the level of productivity in his part of the plant. The president is in turn answerable to the board of directors, and the board of directors is answerable to the stockholders, who have invested their money and expect a profit in return. At each point along the ladder, the specific concerns of individuals are different, but everyone along the way must answer to someone else for his actions. Even the stockholders or owners of the company must answer to the government, and the government is in turn answerable to the people, which brings the accountability full circle.

We have always held that the man who breaks a jewelry-store window and steals a diamond is answerable to the laws of the land. If he is caught, he is held accountable, and he must take the consequences. On the other hand, the man who works hard to save a million dollars, or build a beautiful farm, or earn a college degree is regarded as having the right to enjoy the advantages which accrue to that diligence. Consequences are inextricably tied to behavior. Good behavior is automatically rewarded. Bad behavior is automatically punished. In either case, the underlying concept is that every individual is accountable to society—he is answerable for his own behavior.

As basic as such a concept is to the give-and-take of organized society, still it is being challenged in modern times. I am not sure exactly who is to blame—some say that psychology is the culprit—but there is a theory gaining support in the land that people should not be judged and held answerable for their behavior. If a kid fools around in school, never studies, and a teacher wants to flunk him, it is becoming increasingly popular to say that it isn't the kid's fault. He must have been poorly motivated, the argument goes, so he shouldn't be blamed. The fault must lie not with him but with the educational system. If a man is a chronic and habitual criminal, a ne'er-do-well who has spent most of his life bouncing in and out of jails, it is becoming fashionable to absolve him of any responsibility, blaming society for making him what he is. There must be something basically wrong with a society that would produce such a man, the argument goes, so it isn't fair to hold him accountable for what he has done. A government servant violates the public trust by lying and cheating and covering up his criminality; yet, when he is called to task, he snivels that it was the atmosphere of immorality, or the pressure from his superiors, that caused him to act illegally, and therefore he should not be held accountable.

In this particular mentality, the trick is to find the most convenient scapegoat possible to avoid taking the responsibility for one's own situation. Parents are prime targets; most of the social institutions also serve the purpose well; and, of course, if all else fails, one can always plead, "The devil made me do it!" The thread that runs through all these excuses is that they are smoke screens; they prevent the individual from looking in the mirror at the person who is really responsible for his plight.

B. F. Skinner, whose portrait adorned the cover of *Time* magazine a couple of years ago, has been called the most influential thinker of this half century. He is the psychologist who wrote the book *Beyond Freedom and Dignity,* which the *New York Times* called the most important book of the 1970s. In it Skinner spells out the manifesto of the no-accountability point of view. Man is not responsible for his behavior, Skinner says. He is constantly being manipulated by his environment and all his actions are forced on him by the conditions under which he has experienced life. No matter what he is or does, Skinner says, he could do no differently. Therefore he should not be praised for being "good" just because he engages in good behavior, nor punished for being "bad" when he behaves badly. He is never good or bad; he merely behaves according to the conditions that exist in him and around him.

I am not a behavioral scientist, and I am certainly no authority on the philosophical background of Skinner's viewpoint, but I can emphatically state that, however appealing some may find such a system from a humanistic point of view, a society built on that premise will never work. After a certain period of time, it just will not function. The work will not be done. If no one is answerable to anyone, if all behavior is equally rewarded regardless of how good or bad it is, if no individual is held accountable for his own activity, a society simply cannot continue to function.

It is doubtful that many people actively espouse such an extreme concept of no-accountability. I even doubt that many people in the United States would agree with the socialistic and communistic systems which preach that people should be rewarded according to need, regardless of their output of energy. But many people have succumbed gradually to this seductive spirit of blaming other people for their troubles, finding scapegoats for their own shortcomings, and generally refusing to take full responsibility for their own situation in life.

There are a few principles of accountability that we would do well to remember.

First, *the more one has, the greater his accountability.* That not only makes good sense, but it has scriptural support as well, in the parable of the men with different numbers of talents. Jesus told this story to speak to us about accountability (or stewardship). The man who was given five talents to invest was answerable for the full responsibility of those five talents. "To whom much is given, much is required" (*see* Luke 12:48). If we acknowledge the fact that the things which we have—health, intelligence, opportunity—come from the hand of God, then we must understand that the more we are given to work with, the more we are answerable for. A man of wealth is expected to do more in his financial contributions than a man of modest means. A person of great influence has a greater responsibility for the effect of his life on others than the anonymous guy who has little "clout" in the world. The individual born with a brilliant mind, or great talent of any kind, has a larger responsibility to use it for good than the person of limited ability.

Believe!

But this principle cuts both ways, you see. It takes into account the different levels at which people start in life, and still holds that each man is answerable at the level at which he finds himself. So the man of modest income is still responsible for his use of money, however insignificant it seems to him. The person who has few friends or social contacts still must be answerable for his attitude and his influence, however limited. Helen Keller could easily have concluded that since she was blind and deaf, she was not answerable for her future. She could have insisted that she had been dealt a losing hand in life, and therefore was entitled to lie down and quit. But she didn't. She accepted full responsibility for her life, regardless of her limitations, and made it a useful and productive one. If an individual is born in the ghetto, with no money or motivation, and he finds himself discriminated against at every turn, it might be tempting for him to say, "Well, I have so many disadvantages that I am not responsible for the way my life turns out." He concludes that he has the right to lie down and quit, always blaming his condition on the circumstances of his birth. But he is still answerable for what he does with what he has.

On the whole, the Amway Corporation is made up of people who have caught the vision of taking their own responsibility for their condition in life. There are over two hundred thousand people in Amway who have decided that they want a bigger piece of the economic pie. They want more income. They want to enjoy things that they cannot afford. So instead of staying on their jobs, grumbling and complaining about inflation and that crummy old company for which they work, and decrying the terrible plight they are in, these folks have decided to do something about it. They have given up watching television every night, or that Saturday golf schedule, or that time when they formerly just sat around and did nothing, and they are out selling Amway products, and sharing the Amway program, to make extra money for the things they want but can't afford. Some of them do well at it and some don't do so well. But the point is that they have quit bellyaching about their condition and are trying to *do* something about it. I guess that is why I like them so much. They are people who have been willing to take the responsibility for themselves, regardless of their circumstances, and move forward from where they are.

A second principle of accountability is that *if one is held accountable, he must be given the freedom to make his own choices.* Accountability and freedom go hand in hand. You can't have one without the other. If I hold a manager in our plant responsible for achieving a certain level of production, I must give him the authority to reward or withhold rewards, as he sees fit, in order to get the job done. If I give my son one thousand dollars and tell him to use it for a year and make money with it, I must also give him the freedom to risk it, invest it, use it in whatever way he chooses. If I hold an individual answerable for his economic condition, I must provide a society in which he has the freedom to do a little extra, work a little harder, and be rewarded on the basis of what he produces. I must turn him loose and give him a free hand.

Communist countries pride themselves on their lack of accountability. They have avoided the vicious pressures of dog-eat-dog capitalism, they say, by providing a system in which every man's financial situation is controlled by the state, so he is not answerable to anyone for how well or how poorly he does. To make Russian citizens accountable for themselves, the Soviet government would have to give them the freedom to make money, to invest, to get ahead or fall behind, to conduct their own affairs. Without giving their people freedom of choice, it is impossible for them to be held answerable for the state of their economy.

Once again, the Scriptures teach this principle. God holds every man accountable for his moral behavior, but He also gives to every man a free will. The individual can choose to serve God or not to serve God, to blaspheme or worship, to conduct his affairs in love or in deceit—he is, in short, free to "do his own thing." God guarantees that freedom. He never forces anyone to walk the straight and narrow. But, having that freedom, every individual must then take the responsibility for his behavior, and be directly answerable to God for it.

Similarly, this country and its economic system offers the greatest possible freedom to its citizens. We have free choices in every area of life. The government does not tell a man where to work in America, as it does in many other nations. A man can walk right off one job today and into a different one tomorrow. He doesn't need permission from anyone. He is free to invest money, buy and sell goods and commodities, trade and deal on the open market, offer his services to whoever will buy—he is free to pursue whatever course seems best to him. In this country a man is free to achieve the amount and type of education he wishes. The American government does not tell this person to go to school and this one to work in a factory. He is free to travel as he pleases, to live where he pleases, to embrace whatever religion he pleases. But there accompanies all that freedom the responsibility for every American citizen to take the credit or the blame for whatever he is. With freedom goes accountability. You can't have one without the other.

A third principle to remember is that *accountability must always include evaluation.* In fact, accountability and evaluation are in a certain sense synonymous. If one is to be held responsible for his level of competence, or the quality of work he does, then it is necessary that his performance be evaluated.

One of the first danger signals that indicates this country is sliding toward no-accountability is the cry that goes up in many quarters against evaluation of individual performance. This viewpoint is most apparent in the educational system, where more and more teachers and academic theorists urge the adoption of no-grade policies. Don't give grades, they argue, because the kid who does poorly will be embarrassed and intimidated by a bad mark. Increasingly the classroom is becoming a place where grades are discarded for fear of hurting those who are at the bottom of the totem pole. Unfortunately, it is impossible to recognize and reward excellence without implicitly identifying inferior performance. But if we refuse to recognize the strong for fear of identifying the weak, we will experience a gradual decline in performance across the board. We destroy the incentive for pursuing excellence. We become oriented toward failure, not success. We spend all our time working with the people at the lower end of the scale, and never develop in children the taste for excellence that is so important to individual fulfillment.

I feel as strongly about the unnecessary intimidation of the weaker student as anyone does. I don't like to see anyone shamed or embarrassed. But if a teacher—or a plant supervisor or a coach or whoever—is forbidden to judge the weak, he has no way to reward the strong, and it is impossible to make anyone accountable for his own work.

Many educators propose grade-free systems because they are themselves reluctant to be evaluated. Try to get a schoolteacher to submit voluntarily to any straight-forward system of evaluation by students, peers, or administrators, and you will usually receive a flurry of evasive, hedging replies. Teachers want to make evaluation of their own performance so ambiguous and so inaccessible that it is meaningless. ("Only after twenty years can a teacher's success with a student be analyzed," one educator claims.) The idea is to get away from a system in which he can be directly and routinely judged and held accountable for the quality of his work. In any system of that type, the inferior worker coasts and the superior one loses his incentive.

Certainly schoolteachers are not the only group gravitating toward this nonevaluating posture. The viewpoint appears, thinly disguised, in many other places. Job security, if it means that a man cannot be fired no matter how poorly he performs, can be just another way of avoiding accountability. Automatic, across-the-board pay increases often provide for workers to be rewarded equally, regardless of their competence, and thus nullify the useful-ness of meaningful evaluation. Even quota systems for the employing of ethnic and minority groups can become dodges by which direct evaluation of performance is made meaningless. As this trend con-tinues, it becomes doubly important that we maintain a system of rewards and punishments based on direct evaluation in our schools. It is in the schools that children learn about life; and life, like it or not, is a harsh regimen in which rewards are contingent on behavior. It is a rule of life: one reaps what he sows. One accepts the conse-quences of his behavior. That is not an artifact of capitalism; it is a rule of nature itself. Accountability is woven into the fabric of life, and the sooner our children learn the reality of cause and effect, of reward and punishment, of accepting the natural and inevitable outcomes of one's actions, the better off they are.

We are not doing a child a favor by shielding him from the con-cept of accountability. When he leaves that cozy classroom, where Teacher gave him equal rewards whether he performed well or poorly, where the industrious and the goof-off were evenly praised and scolded, where there was no advantage attached to excellence and no penalty for incompetence—when Junior leaves that class-room to encounter the unblinking, unyielding laws of life, he will be unprepared to answer for himself.

That is no favor to Junior. And that is no favor to the society he lives in. He must believe, as must we all, in accountability, because in the push-and-shove of life we can never escape our responsibility to one another. And in the end, we cannot escape our responsibil-ity to God.

Believe!

...in an Upward Look

Introduction

If there's a word that best describes the American spirit throughout history, it's *optimism*.

This is the land where we believe anyone can do anything. We've always been defined by our belief that tomorrow will be better than today—that our children will be better off than us.

And we've been right! Every generation has led more prosperous lives than the one that came before it. That belief in a brighter future has spurred hundreds of millions of people to improve their lives and the world around them.

But now that positive thinking can be harder to find. No wonder: For the past few decades, we've surrounded ourselves with negativity and resentment.

The traditional media started feeding us nothing but horror stories. The sky is falling; the climate is collapsing; the country is rotten to the core.

And social media? Where to begin! Not only do the algorithms prey on our fears, but nefarious people purposely seek to feed us information that they want us to accept as "truth." It's propaganda on a scale that's almost unimaginable. These people want to make you believe things so that you will act in their best interests, not yours. They'll even censor you—a clear step on the road to despotism. It's terrifying, dangerous, and utterly immoral.

Don't get me wrong. Negativity has always been a fact of life, a basic human temptation. People always find reasons to feel down in the dumps, myself included. It's natural. Things go wrong all the time. But it's also necessary to move past the negativity toward a sunnier outlook.

What's happening now is unnatural. It's designed to trap us, to indoctrinate us, to get us to believe things that aren't good, true, or beautiful. We've entered an era of *permanent pessimism*.

Clearly, it's not working out for us. Mental health problems are soaring, especially among kids. Loneliness is soaring, too. But the worst thing about this permanent pessimism is that it makes us *passive*.

If all you hear is how awful things are, it can be tough to motivate yourself. But it's vital to recognize that you are *not* stuck, and things are *not* as bad as some may want you to believe. In this time of coercion and propaganda, all the claims that others are feeding you are not necessarily true. But what is true is that you can make a difference—that you can always make things better.

The COVID pandemic was a powerful reminder that optimism beats pessimism—that action is the answer to problems.

The pandemic turned the world upside down. Millions of lives were lost and millions more were ruined. Government leaders weren't truthful and treated us as if we were stupid, helpless, or useless. They forced small businesses into bankruptcy, banned people from going to church, and made families watch through windows as their loved ones died. They told us they were doing all the right things and that there was nothing we could do to help. They said we didn't have a choice in the matter.

But they were wrong. We have the God-given power to choose for ourselves. We're the key to finding solutions. And in the pandemic, Americans proved it.

Remember the stories of factory workers who quickly retooled their assembly lines to make protective equipment? Remember how distilleries shifted overnight from making alcohol to hand sanitizer? There were countless examples of people stepping up. They rejected the lie from on high that they should sit back and let the experts handle it.

At Amway, our manufacturing team wanted to help, too. Our community in Grand Rapids was running out of hand sanitizer, especially at hospitals. We didn't make hand sanitizer, but we had the know-how and raw materials. The team of about forty people got together in the newly virtual environment to hammer out how to make a safe, reliable product while protecting our employees. In several days, they had figured it all out and delivered fourteen thousand units of hand sanitizer to the community. They called it "Project Lightspeed."

Our team did this because they said to themselves, "I can make a difference—and I can make it right now."

Talk about positive thinking in a negative time! Now imagine if all of us embraced that same belief in a better future and our own ability to shape it. We can regain that essential belief. And for many people, it starts with a deceptively simple choice.

Put down the phone. Turn off Netflix. When talking heads, influencers, or "experts" try to shake your belief in tomorrow, shake your head and smile, because in your heart, you know better. The sooner we stop letting others get us down, the sooner we'll move ourselves—and our country—up.

After all, this is America, the land of optimism as much as opportunity.

—Doug DeVos

Have you ever noticed how frequently things turn out badly when you expect them to? It seems to me that when I expect something bad to happen, I am never disappointed. If I wait long enough, eventually things will turn out as badly as I had feared.

But I have also noticed that the same principle works in reverse: if I expect good things to happen, they usually do! All I have to do is wait long enough, and expect good things to happen strongly enough, and it's not long before it all turns out the way I had hoped.

Life is that way. It tends to respond to our outlook, to shape itself to meet our expectations. Any psychologist will tell you that if a boy is called "thief" often enough, eventually he will steal something; if a student is constantly called "stupid," he will soon begin to behave stupidly; if an occasion is dreaded passionately enough, it certainly will prove to be as bad as its anticipation. The events of life, in their endless flux and flow, seem somehow to shake out pretty much as we expect them to. There is enough good and bad in everyone's life, enough sorrow and happiness, enough joy and pain, that any one of us can find ample excuse to look up or look down, to laugh or to cry, to see the world as a blessing or a curse.

I believe in an upward look! Given the option to read life however I choose, I believe in underlining the positive passages with a bright red pencil and skipping over the negative ones with barely a glance. I am an optimist. I know that sorrow exists, that life is not an unbroken delight; but I have been alive for over forty years, and on the balance I find the good in life more impressive than the bad. In the words of the old song, I have chosen to "accentuate the positive" and "eliminate the negative."

Charles Simmons, one of those powerful pulpit ministers of the early nineteenth century, said it this way:

Give me a positive character, with a positive faith, positive opinions and positive actions…rather than a negative character, with a doubting faith, wavering opinions, undecided actions and faintness of heart!

For a person who wants to be happy and productive, an upward look is not just a luxury. It is absolutely imperative. Why? Because the way one looks at life determines how he feels, how he performs, how well he gets along with other people. Negative thoughts and attitudes feed on themselves. They pile up higher and higher until the world actually becomes the grim place that they describe.

One time I drove my car into a service station to get some gasoline. It was a beautiful day and I was feeling fine. As I walked into the station, a young chap standing there said, rather unexpectedly, "How do you feel?"

I said, "I feel wonderful."

"You look sick," he said. Get the picture: this fellow wasn't a medical doctor; he wasn't an internist; he wasn't a male nurse.

I answered him, maybe a little less confidently this time, "No, I feel fine. I never felt better."

He said, "Well, you don't look so good. Your color is bad. You look yellow."

Well, I left that gas station and before I had driven a block I stopped the car and looked in the mirror to see how I felt! After I got home I kept checking for pale color, yellow jaundice, something, anything! I thought, maybe I don't feel all right after all. Maybe I have a bad liver. Maybe I'm sick and just don't know it.

The next time I went to that gas station I figured out what the problem was: they had just painted the station a sick-looking yellow, and everybody who went into the place developed a ghastly yellow look!

Believe!

The point is that I had let one comment from one total stranger change my whole attitude for the rest of that day. He told me I looked sick, and before I knew it I was actually *feeling* sick! It is amazing how powerful a single negative thought can be.

On the other hand, almost any woman whom I have ever asked will admit that she has a dress or two hanging in her closet that she has worn only once, and never reached for again. And the reason that the dress was never worn a second or third time was that on the one occasion that she wore it not a person complimented it. No one noticed. Nobody walked up and said, "Oh, Janet, what a beautiful dress!" She didn't need the whole crowd to stand up and cheer, but if only one or two people had said, "My, that looks nice on you," she would have practically worn that thing out, instead of letting it hang there and gather dust.

Few things in the world are more powerful than a positive push. A smile. A word of optimism and hope. A "You can do it" when things are tough. That upward look that refuses to dwell on the negative, but keeps pointing to things that are positive and strong.

America has traditionally been a nation of an upward look. We in this country have always been eager to see the world as a positive, hopeful place and to see ourselves and our fellow citizens as favorably as the facts would allow. I am afraid that in the last few years we may have been losing that positive, optimistic approach. We seem to be entering an era when the critic, the naysayer, the prophet of despair has become the hero of the day.

I noticed not long ago that one nationally famous critic spoke on a large college campus and delivered his usual speech on what was wrong with everybody and everything, and the students stood up and cheered him. He became a hero merely by ripping up the leaders and institutions and traditions of the day.

We spend too much of our time looking down, finding fault, picking to pieces our systems and institutions, our colleges and churches, and—worst of all—each other. If we spend all our time finding fault, we will not have the human energy or the courage or the strength to try to solve the problems that genuinely afflict our institutions and organizations. The student who spends all his time finding fault with his college usually never gets around to helping it become a better college. If a man has a good friend, and all he does is tell that friend his faults, he will not be able to build the person up constructively or make him a better person.

In either case, the individual becomes a full-time critic and fault-finder. He becomes so obsessed with shouting about the problem that he never attempts to solve it. Finding problems is not difficult— problems are everywhere. To glorify the critic while ignoring the much greater contribution of the man who copes with and solves the problem is a monstrous injustice.

In New York City a new stage play opens on Broadway. People have worked and sweated blood over that play for months or even years. Investors were sought, scripts were written, music was composed, the theater was rented, actors and actresses learned their lines and rehearsed for weeks. Finally the play opens. Scores of people pour themselves into it—stagehands, directors, makeup crew, musicians, ushers, and curtain boys—all working hard to create something special for their audience.

But out there in the crowd somewhere sit four or five critics, and if they don't like the play, it is usually finished. It's done. On opening night the actors sit around in some crummy little joint off Broadway and wait for the morning papers to come out, and they read what a good job or what a terrible job they did, and they know that on the basis of that criticism from four or five people the show will fold in a matter of weeks, or go on to a long run.

There is nothing wrong with that so long as society doesn't make a hero out of the critic. The critic has his place. He has a legitimate function, and he has a job to do. But when we reach the place where we praise the critic more for his "rip job" than we do the playwright who wrote the play, then the premium is being placed on the wrong job. It is much easier to criticize than to create. Much easier to point out the flaw in a product than to produce the goods. Much easier to tear something down than to build it. When we worship the critic, we eventually develop a nation of critics, all of them unwilling to put it all on the line and attempt to create. Rather than expose themselves to the jeers of the cynics, they do nothing at all.

Don't get me wrong. I think critics are necessary as long as we keep their role in perspective. It is a disaster to continue to focus not on men who do things, but on men who find fault with those who do things. We discredit the people who are problem solvers and praise those who point out the problem. That is the surest way I know to develop a nation of professional bellyachers! That approach produces a generation of young people who sit around discussing the deplorable shape of the world, shooting down anyone who is out there trying to do something about it.

Ralph Nader has never built a car. He has only a limited idea of the complexity of mass-producing a modern automobile at a price that ten million Americans every year can afford to pay. It doesn't take too much savvy to find fault with your car—or your house, your husband, or your wife. Anybody can do that. What really impresses me is not the problems that cars have, but the nearly miraculous accomplishment that every finished automobile represents when it rolls off the assembly line. I marvel at the people who work in those factories with all that racket and noise. I marvel at the way they get all those pieces made in plants all over the country and put them together. Somebody in Timbuktu makes the grill, and somebody else makes the emblem, somebody else makes the seat covers, and someone else gets all the stereo jacks to go in the right place. Somebody puts the wiring harnesses together and someone else gets the strip of metal just right on the steering wheel and tests the shock absorbers to make sure the ride is smooth. From plants and little shops all over the country somebody organizes all that and gets it together so that cars come sliding off that line like a cordwood, each one capable of going a hundred miles an hour with a self-contained heating-and-cooling system, dozens of built-in safety devices, and a ride more comfortable than folks dreamed of a few years back.

And it all comes together like clockwork, because most of the time most of the people are doing one heck of a good job. The stereo system hooks up to the rear speaker just right and the seats match the paint job; the chrome is straight and the right tires are on the right models. Thousands of pieces come together and—wonder of wonder—the whole thing works!

To me the man who keeps all that going is the real hero. The guy who figured out how to get a steel belt inside a fiber-glass tire is a hero. That ingenious fellow who designed a muffler that lasts twice as long as the old one is a hero. Ralph Nader is a fine fellow, I'm sure. He has a part to play in our society. He is a watchdog, a professional critic, an important person to have around. But is he the hero of our little scenario? Not in my book, he's not! The real heroes are the men who have been providing America with goods and services for seventy years—the executives, scientists, designers, and workmen and housewives who make something good and positive. Without them there is nothing at all.

I don't dislike Ralph Nader. I just get tired of his constantly talking things down, constantly finding fault. And I am concerned that the attention and space in the media given to such men is creating a national climate of criticism and cynicism that will ultimately discourage the creative and the optimistic.

If the "downward look" were confined to a few nationally known critics, that would not be so bad. But sometimes ordinary people carry around with them such a negative attitude that, like the sick-yellow service station, their jaundiced view of life affects everyone around them. Just listen to the conversation today on the job, or in the coffee shop, or on the bus going to work. There is always someone who wants to talk about how things are. First it is the economy. Then it is the crime problem. Then the fact that kids are less respectful than they ought to be, or that there are too many reruns on TV, or that prices are rising too fast for a man to keep up. A man named Thomas Shepherd calls this kind of person a member of the "disaster lobby." They constantly look back to the "good ol' days" and moan for them to return. But was life really better in those days? One hundred and fifty years ago, Shepherd points out, the average life expectancy was 38 years, the work week was 72 hours, the average pay was $275 per year. Housewives worked 98 hours a week, and there were no dishwashers or vacuum cleaners. The average person never in his lifetime heard the sound of an orchestra or traveled more than two hundred miles from his birthplace. Those were *good* ol' days? We may as well admit it—things are getting better. We are better off in most ways than any generation before us and things are bound to keep on improving.

I recently had some high-school kids on my boat, sailing on Lake Michigan. It happened that at the same time we had a crew of astronauts on the moon. One of these high-school boys said to me, "Well, that's a waste of money up there. We should have spent that money here on earth, where things are in such bad shape."

I answered him, "It was four hundred forty-five million dollars we spent on that project of putting men on the moon. What do you think we should have done with it?"

His answer came right back: "I think we should work on the poverty problem."

"Fine," I said. "How would you solve it?"

That stopped him for a minute. He replied slowly, "Well, I don't know."

I said, "Tell me how much money you need to solve the poverty problem and how you'll spend it and I'll get it for you." He asked me where I was going to get the money. "You give me a solution," I told him, "and I'll get you the money, I promise." That started a pretty lively discussion, because finally that boy was forced to quit talking in vague, general complaints and look specifically at the thing he was calling the "poverty problem." He began to think about solutions instead of merely dwelling on the problems. He put himself in the place of the fixer rather than constantly serving as the critic. And when he did that, we spent the rest of the day in a healthy, constructive discussion of the issues about which he was concerned.

It is easy never to get that far, never to get the level of one's sight off the ground and up into the sky. The richness of life, the love and joy and exhilaration of life can be found only with an upward look.

This is an exciting world. It is cram-packed with opportunity. Great moments wait around every corner. It is a world that deserves an upward look. We have heard enough from the critics and the naysayers, the cynics whose vocabularies have not progressed beyond the word *no*, the rip artists whose talent for seeing sore spots has made instant experts and heroes of them. I believe in life with a large yes and a small no. I believe that life is good, that people are good, that God is good. And I believe in affirming every day that I live, proudly and enthusiastically, that life in America under God is a positive experience!

Believe!

...in Free Enterprise

Introduction

How do you solve the biggest problems in our country? Poverty. Addiction. Crime. Bad schools. The list goes on.

These problems are big. Surely, we need big solutions—maybe from big government, or big ideas from experts, or something or someone else that's big and bold. Right?

This may very well be the biggest lie in twenty-first-century America.

As a country, we've forgotten that progress comes from people— and not just "powerful" or "smart" people. Progress comes from seemingly ordinary people, because all of us are capable of extraordinary things.

You may be thinking: *Okay, here goes another anti-government rant.* So let's take government out of the picture for a moment.

Who do you think makes the biggest impact on our economy? Big businesses or small businesses?

Most people say big businesses—the ones on Wall Street. But actually, small businesses do far more to lift up America.

Small businesses create two out of every three net new jobs. Small businesses produce sixteen times more patents per employee than big businesses. Main Street is crushing Wall Street on basically every metric!

Why do small businesses do so much more than people realize? They aren't bogged down by bureaucracy. They're creative and nimble and laser-focused on a specific thing. In short, small businesses are closer to the problems they're trying to solve, so it's easier for them to find solutions. And this same insight holds true pretty much everywhere.

If we're going to tackle the big challenges in our country, we should start as close to the problems as possible—the overlooked people in the unexpected places.

This is the essence of free enterprise. It's not simply about economics. It's about entrepreneurship, in the broadest sense. Entrepreneurship—in business and communities alike—is about unleashing every person's innate skills, for the benefit of society at large.

At its core, free enterprise is built on a deep belief in people. That's why this principle spoke so much to Dad and Jay. For them, free enterprise was summed up in a display at the 1964 World's Fair called the "Ten Pillars of Economic Wisdom." In fact, they liked the display so much, they bought it. The pillars now stand outside of Amway World Headquarters, declaring that "millions of progress-seeking individuals" are infinitely more innovative and creative than a "state-planned society."

This is a truth of history and not just in business. All of us are collectively smarter than some of us—and we're certainly smarter than the so-called "experts." In our complicated world, we don't need to outsource creative thinking to those "experts." Just the opposite: We need everyone to tackle problems from every angle. Your experiences and skills are different from mine. You'll find solutions that I can't even comprehend!

Here's another way to put it: progress comes from the bottom up, not the top down. America's been trying top-down for decades, especially in government. How's it working? Not well! So why do we keep trying even bigger one-size-fits-all solutions? It's the definition of insanity.

Every generation has a tendency to think that top-down is the best way forward. Over a hundred years ago, the politicians in DC backed a bigshot team of experts to build the world's first airplane. The government gave them huge amounts of money and the media fawned over them. It was a sure bet, right? Surely the experts would get it right.

But the government backed the wrong horse.

Shortly thereafter, another airplane flew first. You know, the one built by two bicycle repairmen named Wilbur and Orville Wright. No one ever expected them to do that. But they beat the government in the race to flight.

A lot has changed since the early 1900s. But our spirit of entrepreneurship endures with incredible results.

Today, the private company SpaceX is far more impressive than government-run NASA. While politicians are obsessed with expensive wind and solar power that only work part of the day, private innovators have created nuclear reactors that work all the time, are small enough to fit in cars, and pose no safety risk whatsoever. Beyond the economy, there's a nonprofit called The Phoenix that's more than twice as effective as traditional treatments when it comes to beating addiction.

The list goes on! Whether it's in business or civil society, the American people still have the endless capacity for solving big problems.

You know who's best suited to keep artificial intelligence on the straight and narrow? You.

You know who's capable of transforming the local school system that's failing so many kids? You.

And you know who has the power to lift up your community, no matter the challenges it faces? You guessed it—you.

Sure, those challenges are big. Huge, even. But we have an even bigger weapon: The genius of 340 million Americans who've never met an unsolvable problem.

—Doug DeVos

IF YOU ASKED ME WHAT IMPORTANT BLESSING Americans most take for granted, I would have a surprising answer for you. It's not the air we breathe, or the churches we attend, or the sun that comes up every morning. Not the love of family and neighbors. Not our health or political freedom. The most grandly ignored blessing of American life is our system of free enterprise.

"Capitalism" has become virtually a dirty word in this generation, and that's a dirty shame!

Unfortunately, words like "free enterprise," "profit," and "capitalism" conjure up visions of money-hungry industrialists greedily stuffing dollars into their pockets while the poor masses become more and more destitute. Free enterprise is fast becoming the all-purpose scapegoat of this half century. The critics will tell you that all the evils of the 1970s are laid at its door. The air and streams are polluted because of capitalism, people are poor because of capitalism, wars are fought because of capitalism. The free-enterprise system is evil, their argument goes, and it poisons the whole society.

What ignorance! What foolish, unfortunate ignorance! The truth of the matter is that the free-enterprise system is the greatest single source of our country's economic success, and its best hope for surviving the demands of this chaotic century. It is time for this generation of Americans to believe once again in free enterprise, to espouse it, to teach it to our young as a positive blessing.

Too many people consider a country's economic system irrelevant to its politics, religious life, and other cultural characteristics. That is a dangerous error. The economic system of a nation is the backdrop against which all else unfolds; it sets the stage for the entire life of a country. Many Americans ignore the blessings of free enterprise because they consider the whole issue irrelevant—a matter for the economists and the political scientists to quibble over. They wear color-coordinated clothes to air-conditioned, carpeted offices and plants, drive luxury automobiles down superhighways to spacious homes set on landscaped lawns, sit down to steak dinners before retiring to king-size beds—and hardly give a thought to the system that makes it all possible. They listen to the news on four channels, worship at whatever church they choose, give to their favorite charities, and wonder if maybe socialism *is* a better way, after all. They hear an ill-informed politician with an ax to grind berate the evils of that monstrous, dog-eat-dog capitalistic system, and wonder if maybe he might be right.

I want to challenge you to believe in free enterprise—because it *does* matter that you believe in it, understand it, and know what it is and is not.

Very simply put, free enterprise happens when the freedom of people is recognized as an inherent right stemming from the Creator, and that freedom is safeguarded (as ours is) in the structure of the government organization. In the free enterprise system, the manufacturer or businessman owns his own tools, risks his own money, sets his own prices, makes his own decisions, and makes or loses money depending on how well he provides the public with a product or service which it wants at a price it is willing to pay. Unless that company does something criminal, or violates the public interest, the government should leave him alone to pursue his interests.

The only real alternative to free enterprise is socialism or, in the extreme, communism. Under these systems the government owns the tools and factories, sets the prices, employs the workers, and provides the public with the product at a price which the government sets.

But between free enterprise and outright socialism is the condition toward which the United States is now gravitating—that of a constantly increasing governmental interference in business, where government sets more and more regulations, makes more and more decisions, owns more and more of the businesses, and slowly squeezes the corporation out of the picture.

The crucial way that an economic system must be judged is by its productive output. What does it provide for the people? What level of life does it make possible for them? Compared on that basis, free enterprise is clearly superior to alternative economic systems. Over the last two hundred years this country has outproduced any other country in the world, hands down. It has provided for its people more material goods than any other system in history.

Consider these figures from the *New York Times:* in the United States a medium-sized automobile costs about 100 days wages; in Moscow it costs about 1,000 days wages. In the United States a small refrigerator costs about 32 hours of work; in Moscow it costs about 343 hours. An average washing machine costs 53 hours here against 204 hours in the Soviet Union. Color television sets cost the equivalent of 147 hours for the American worker; in Moscow the price is 1,110 hours. The comparisons go on and on, and always the result is the same: the American system gives its workers a far greater reward for their work than does socialism or communism, its most prominent economic alternatives. And that is the ultimate test of an economic system: the degree to which it yields returns to the individual on his labor, whether that labor is by the sweat of his brow or by his managerial or creative skills.

The United States has only 6 percent of the world's population and we have about 7 percent of the land surface of the world. But, despite the fact that we are so small in comparison to the rest of the world, we as American citizens own 45 percent of all the automobiles, 60 percent of all the telephones, 30 percent of all the radios, and 80 percent of the television sets! On the production side, this country produces 25 percent of all the steel, 40 percent of the electric power, 50 percent of the corn, 60 percent of the natural gas, 30 percent of the beef, and 40 percent of all the aluminum in the world! And all of that by 6 percent of the world's population!

Believe!

Of course, any time someone begins to quote statistics like that which show the overwhelming superiority of the American free-enterprise system, the critics start hollering about something they call the "quality of life." The "quality of life" is somehow lower under capitalism, they insist, even in the face of all these material goods. But I have found that it is difficult for people to worry about the quality of life when they are hungry. There is no concern for good books, good music, symphony orchestras, or a provocative intellectual climate when a man must work eighty hours a week to keep warm and fed and under a roof at night. When a man spends all day struggling to sustain himself, he has no time to worry about the "quality of life."

The truth is that in America more people can read, write, and speak the language than anywhere else in the world. More people go to church. More people receive a college education. More people have more time and more money for the enrichment of their lives beyond the workaday demands of scratching out a living. The advanced medical research of this country, the enormous recreational programs for young people, the hospitals and churches, the schools and museums, the organizations that send millions of dollars overseas every month—all these are possible only because under a free-enterprise system there is enough material wealth *left over* from survival needs to do all these things. There is no United Fund in Russia because nobody has anything to give but the government!

Still the system is criticized. Another popular blast leveled at free enterprise is that under such a system there are too many wealthy people, too many who have too much. Once, when I was speaking on free enterprise at a college, a young man challenged me about the Cadillac I was driving at the time. "If you're really concerned about the poor," he said, "why don't you give up that Cadillac you're driving and drive an old car, one that will just get you where you want to go?" What that student inaccurately believed was that if the rich have less the poor will have more. That is not the case. If those who have material wealth have less, then everyone has less. If you want the caboose to catch up with the locomotive, you don't do it by stopping the train. If the rich become poor, everyone has less.

I explained to the young man that I provided work for lots of men by buying that Cadillac. For me to be poor would not make any one of them richer. If the farmer gets less for his produce, the food doesn't get cheaper; it gets more expensive, because the farmer, having no incentive, produces less food. If America were poorer, the poorest country in Africa would be no better off. We all would have less. The only way for there to be more material wealth in the purse of the have-nots is for there to be more goods produced, and the only way to produce more is to provide incentives for people to work harder and more efficiently. And any time those incentives are provided, there will be some people who have more than others, because some will always work a little harder, do a little more to get more for themselves.

Certainly it is the responsibility of a nation to see that the rich do not take advantage of the poor, or abuse the poor, but to suggest that if the rich had less the poor would have more is a fallacy. There simply would *be* less. Those who hail socialism as a great system because in it all men are equal are right up to a certain degree. Under socialism all men are equal—they are equally poor! That is the record of history. It is clear and irrefutable.

What accounts for the massive superiority of American production over that of other systems? It is not the presence of natural resources; for, rich as our country is in natural wealth, it is easily matched and even surpassed by others. It is not that American people are smarter, or stronger, or more industrious, though that would be a pleasant vanity to entertain if it were true. It is not that we have been at it longer, because our two hundred-year history makes us practically a johnny-come-lately on the world scene. What, then, is the secret of our phenomenal productive power?

It is the system.

Believe!

We have a system which allows the people to own privately the tools of production, and one which allows the man who produces more to get ahead of the man who produces less. The matter of incentive for greater productivity will come up again later. For now, let's look at the importance of private ownership of the tools.

It is the tools, after all, that make the difference. A tool may be a hammer or a steam shovel or a tractor-trailer truck or a computer or a conveyor belt. It is an instrument which a man uses that enables him to produce more with his output of energy. All over the world, men are roughly equal in energy, intelligence, and willingness to work. Italians, Indians, Czechs, Russians, Argentines, all are pretty much the same in their raw energy and ability. But a man with a tool can do more than a man without a tool. A man can work hard for eight hours digging a hole in the ground with his bare hands. A man with a pick, in the same amount of time, can dig a much bigger hole without working any harder. And a man with a bulldozer can dig a far bigger hole yet. That doesn't mean that he is a better man, or that he has any greater human value—it just means that he has a better tool.

The farmer in Spain who walks behind one old mule with a little plow and plows one acre a day is no less a person than the farmer in Kansas who plows a thousand acres a week sitting in a high-powered tractor. Once I was in Peru and saw men walking around with lumber on their backs. They carried that stuff on their backs, all bent over, from one place to another. They can move perhaps one hundred pounds ten miles in a day. One of our truck drivers climbs into the cab of a tractor-trailer rig, adjusts his cushion, slips an eight-track tape into the dash, and rolls down the highway at fifty-five miles an hour hauling thousands of pounds, day and night, without stopping. Is that truck driver a better man? No, but he has a better tool, so he produces more and lives better as a result.

It is only when one sees some of the modern tools that he can fully appreciate how powerfully a tool can change a man's ability to produce. Modern technology can put tools into a man's hands that enable him to outproduce hundreds of men without those tools. And a whole society of men with such powerful tools reaps the benefit of a work force comparable to billions of workers without tools. At our plant in Ada, Michigan, for example, we produce aerosol cans. I used to test the cans by hand, one at a time. Now we have an assembly line that produces them and cranks them out at the rate of three cans *per second!* Those cans come off the line in a blur—powerfully impressive tool! We have a computer there at Amway, and they tell me that it can print out information at the rate of eleven hundred lines per minute—that's the equivalent of one secretary typing over twenty-seven thousand words per minute, or a book-length novel in three minutes!

The list of examples is endless. It takes no time at all to recognize that it is the tools that man has which have brought him from the more primitive forms of life to the relatively rich culture of today. And the economic system which optimizes the development and use of tools will be the most productive system.

And that is exactly the point at which free enterprise has any socialistic system hopelessly beaten. The American Economic Foundation came up with a formula that explains just how tools are the pivotal element of an economy. The formula has been around for years, and I enjoy repeating and explaining it when I speak on free enterprise. It goes this way: $MMW = NR + HE \times T$—Man's material welfare equals natural resources plus human energy multiplied by *tools*. All that man has of a material nature comes from the earth in some form (natural resources), but it must be converted into usable form by his own effort (human energy), whether it is physical work or mental work of whatever.

All countries have natural resources. All countries have human energy. But all countries do not have an equivalent share of material wealth. The main reason is that in some systems the people are allowed to own the tools, and in those systems the tools are better cared for and more efficiently used. In addition, those same systems give people extra benefits for developing new tools, so more new tools are developed.

People take better care of things that belong to them. That is human nature. If you don't believe it, just rent your house to someone for a year and see how well he takes care of it—or vice versa. If I don't own something, it just seems less important that I take care of it.

One day I was with some guys coming out of Los Angeles on a crowded freeway early in the morning. The smog was bad; the freeway was crowded. We got frustrated waiting to get into a line of traffic, and finally I said, "Aw, cut on in, John, it's a rented car anyway!" Suddenly it occurred to me that I would never have been so casual about banging up my own automobile. If you don't own it, you don't take care of it as well. And that is exactly the problem they have in Russia. The state owns all the tools, the factories, the buildings, the means of production, and nobody takes care of them. A psychologist, Albert Bandura, once said, "No single snowflake in an avalanche ever feels responsible." That is how it is with a sense of responsibility for tools owned by the state. It belongs to everybody, so nobody feels responsible. The tools of production—the key to material wealth—are abused and neglected and get only half the life and efficiency of privately owned tools in America.

The other aspect of the tool factor in comparing the two systems is that, in a free-enterprise system, the development of new tools is rewarded. Suppose you spent months and years working in your basement at night to invent a better plow, or a more efficient vacuum cleaner, or a sharper pair of scissors. How would you react if, when you finished that new tool, the government took it from you and said, "Thanks a lot, but this new invention now belongs to the people," and took it from you without paying you for your years of hard work and ingenuity? You would be angry, of course. You would be disillusioned and bitter and would be determined never to waste your time again developing a new tool. You worked hard while others were sleeping, watching TV, having a good time, and you got nothing for it. And so it is that in a socialistic system the incentive to develop and own new tools is squashed, and tools are developed with less frequency than in a free-enterprise system.

In America if you invented that new machine it would be yours. You would be free to sell it to the highest bidder. Or you could manufacture it and sell it by the millions. In either case, the patent law would protect your right to reap the benefit from your work. You would make money, thereby sharing the payoff of that better tool which increased someone's productive efficiency. And so you, and others like you, would be willing to do a little extra, work a little harder, explore your new ideas and convert them into reality, and as a result the whole society becomes more and more productive, and everyone lives a little better, especially those who have the initiative to go that extra step.

Free enterprise is really that simple. It is a system in which the individual has a right to conduct his business in whatever way he chooses, and keep the benefits of his work. That system is threatened whenever government burdens the businessman with rules and regulations, tells him how to operate his business, and generally increases his cost of producing goods. In the United States today the freedom of businesses to pursue their affairs is being severely limited by a flood of nit-picking, unnecessary regulations. That becomes a real danger, because as government gets more and more involved in the job of running the nation's businesses, the tools of production come more into the control of the government and not of the people. Already in this country we have people yelling for the government to take over the oil industry, the railroads, the telephone systems, medical treatment, you name it.

When that happens, when the tools of this great industrial nation become the property of government and not of individual owners, those tools will be wasted and abused.

Look at public housing. Buildings built to last thirty years are run-down and ramshackle after five years. They belong to everybody and they belong to nobody. But if I own a tool, and I am going to reap the benefits of its use, you'd better believe I will take care of it and use it well.

The bottom line is this: when the state controls the tools of production, it controls the people. They become slaves. By withholding the tools from them the state can reduce them to the level of primitive man; by saying when and how and for what purposes those tools may be used, it can control the life of every man.

When Fidel Castro took over Cuba he marched in and took control of the means of production. The young people were elated—they had finally overthrown that dirty scoundrel Batista, that capitalistic pig! Now the "people" owned the cane, the plantations, the refineries. All would be sweetness and light. But when the time came to cut the cane—which is hard, dirty work—some of the students said, "Uh, if you don't mind, Fidel, we don't want to cut the cane."

And Fidel said, "Brothers, together we march forward to cut the cane."

And again they said, "But we don't like to cut cane."

So Fidel said, "You *will* cut the cane! You will either cut the cane or go to jail." So they cut the cane. That is the way the economic life of Cuba has been managed ever since, and likewise in other anticapitalistic countries. The standard of living has just kept going down, until there are more and more poor people, not fewer.

The record of history is clear. The free-enterprise system has outperformed, outproduced any other in the world. It has provided more goods for more people, more jobs in better conditions, more wealth for less labor. It has left people free to control their own lives, to produce at the rate they choose, and reap the benefits of their labor.

It is a gift of God to us, and we should understand it, embrace it, and believe in it.

Believe!

...in Human Dignity

Introduction

Who are you? This shouldn't be a hard question. My answer is that I'm a child of God. I'm a husband and a father and now a grandfather too. I'm also a businessman, a sailor, and an often disappointed yet eternally hopeful Detroit Lions fan. And of course, I'm a proud American. I'm so many things. All of them add up to who I am. Even then, I'm more than the sum of my parts. So are you.

But ask someone who doesn't know me about who I am, and you probably won't get that answer. They're more likely to say: Doug's a successful businessman. Maybe they'll say I'm from a successful family, too. It happens to be true. But is that really the whole truth about who I am?

We live in a time of labeling people. We label each other by skin color—white, black, brown, you name it. We label each other by who we like—gay or straight or something else. We label people by income—rich or poor. Or even political party—Republican or Democrat.

Regardless of the label we use, we're making one of the oldest mistakes around. Of course these things are part of who we are. But at the end of the day, they only describe us. They don't define us.

People are more than their skin color or chromosomes or political party. We're human beings made in the image and likeness of God. We all share the same human dignity.

Believe!

No one has made this point better than Dr. Seuss in his children's book about Star-Belly Sneetches. It features a salesman who preyed on differences among the fictional creatures. Some had stars on their bellies while others didn't, and he pitted them against each other. For those who didn't have stars, he sold them a machine that gave them one. For those who did have stars, he sold them a machine that took them off. As soon as the Sneetches paid him for one machine, they got jealous and paid him to go through the other machine, too—a vicious cycle that only ended when the salesmen left with all their money. Thankfully, in the end, the Sneetches realized they were all the same—stars or not.

We need a similar realization in America today. Our society shows that when you confuse what defines us with what describes us, things get ugly really fast.

Put simply, we're pitting people against each other. It's a never-ending struggle to gain power over some people instead of attempting to empower every person. We have to pull ourselves out of this spiral. And that starts by recognizing some fundamental truths.

First and foremost: You are unique. No one can make you better. You're the only one who can make the most of your life. Don't let anyone take that away from you.

Second: We all deserve equal rights and opportunity. We're all born with gifts and talents. No one's born a victim or an oppressor. Have faith in yourself. You are empowered to direct your future. You make the decisions for you. You're in control, not someone else.

Third: We all deserve the chance to rise. Does everyone start in the same place? Of course not. But within our communities, we can always help people make up lost ground. We just have to do it right, with a firm reliance on human dignity. The solution is *never* to lower standards later in life. The solution is *always* to lift someone up earlier.

If human dignity means anything, it's that no one should get ahead by causing someone else to fall behind.

Years ago, Amway hired a consultant to help us develop our recruitment of new Amway distributors. He was immediately concerned that we let anyone—yes, anyone—join the team and start building their business. He told Dad and Jay that Amway needed to be more selective. We should screen prospects to make sure they have the right educational background, presentation skills, and sales experience. We should only recruit the best and not be bothered with those who may not succeed.

Dad and Jay had a simple question for him: Who do you want to leave out?

They fired him immediately because he completely missed the point. The consultant wanted us to only care about what described people, not what defined them. But years of Amway experience have demonstrated that those who have all the "right" qualifications may not be successful, while those with no qualifications can achieve incredible success. They have the character and drive—the things that really count.

Doesn't twenty-first-century America try to do the same thing as that consultant? Aren't we told that some people are better than others just because of their appearances, lifestyle, or success?

It's never true and it will never be true. You were created to be uniquely you and you have value simply because of that powerful fact. Forget what you see in someone. Dig deeper to discover who people really are from the inside out.

After all, the real answer is always more interesting and exciting than you may expect.

—Doug DeVos

THERE IS A LINE FROM AN OLD SONG that declares that love "makes the world go 'round." At the risk of sounding hopelessly antiromantic, I would like to revise that line slightly: it is respect that makes the world go 'round. The most important commodity in the world is respect for the individual man.

When I say "respect for the individual man," I mean it in terms of specific, day-to-day attitudes and behavior, not respect for man in some abstract sense of "mankind," but an active, daily awareness of the worth and value of every man, regardless of his situation or station in life, color, creed, or whatever else. I believe that every man on earth is a creature of God, that he is here for a purpose, and that he is worthy of my respect as a human being.

The thing that stands in the way of respect for all God's children is the whole system of pigeonholes and categories into which we push people. We talk about a man according to whether he went to this school or that school, has this degree or that degree, works at this job or another job, according to the car he drives, or the house he lives in, or the accent of his voice. And too often we are so busy relating to him in these little air-tight categories that we never get around to seeing him as a fellow creature on this planet, a brother under the skin, a human individual of worth and destiny. Respect—that is the key. And it is difficult to have real respect for a man if I can only see the cut of his clothes or the color of his money.

We have these sacred labels that we worship. This job is "professional" and that one is not. This person is worthy and that one is disadvantaged. Things such as higher education have emerged as a kind of national mania, so that a person is hardly considered worthy of notice unless he has a college degree. We seem to say, "I don't want to know who you are, what you can do, what the condition of your heart is, what strengths you have, or what obstacles you have overcome—first I want to see your college degree!"

Another category system that has grown equally out of proportion to its real importance is money. It is possible for a worthless fool to have money—just as it is possible for him to get a college degree. Other things are often more important in judging a man than either of these, but too often people are shoved to the background without a chance to show their real worth unless they have money or a college education. They feel like the comedian Rodney Dangerfield, whose trademark is the complaint, "I don't get no respect!" And they have every right to feel that way.

A couple of years ago I was at a symposium on vocational education held by the governor of a northern state. I sat through the meeting all day with men who had doctor's degrees and great experience in higher education; and all day long I heard a stream of comments which showed a deep, pervasive, perhaps even unintentional disrespect for the out-of-work laborer—the very men whom these experts were supposed to be trying to help. I heard lines like this one: "Well, I hope through vocational education we can make these men good citizens." Or, "Maybe at least we can make a good carpenter out of him." Or one of the experts would say, "Well, he would still be *just* a plumber, but ...."

Finally, I was tired of hearing it. I happened to be the speaker that night, and I opened my remarks by saying, "Gentlemen, with all humility, I would like to say that unless you can develop some respect for the men you're trying to educate, you'd better stop trying to get the job done. You're looking down your noses from your Ph.D. towers and somehow you're trying to find some little niche in society for the poor fellow who isn't bright enough, in your opinion, to get a college degree."

Make no mistake about it, I am all for college education and all for people having lots of money and all for every kind of advancement that anyone can make. But I don't think we should draw up this set of categories and say, in effect, to 100 million Americans, "Since you don't have any of these traditional symbols of success, you are nothing." We have Ph.D.s working for us in the Amway Corporation, chemists and lawyers and computer experts. I recognize the value of their training and their expertise. I salute the kid who scratches and claws and digs his way through college and graduate school and becomes a doctor or a scientist or whatever. But I don't think that he is one bit better than the fifteen hundred honest, hardworking men and women who run the machinery, push the brooms, and do the production-line labor back in the plant. I respect the truck driver who does his thing well.

I resent anyone who says about a non-professional worker, "He is *just* a mechanic," or "*just* a salesman," or *just* anything—he is a warm, giving, highly complex human being, cast in the image of God Himself, who is doing his job with pride and competence. He is the backbone of this country; he is the guy who gets the job done; he is the unsung hero of our whole society—and when I think of all he has accomplished, I practically burst with pride in his achievement and respect for what he is.

One summer my family and I were living at a cottage, and we had a garbage man who was the best garbage man I have ever seen in my life. He was fantastic. He was there at half-past six in the morning; you could set your clock by him. He didn't throw the trash can, didn't heave it in the general direction of the truck and hope it got there. And after he emptied the cans, he didn't sling the lids at them and see how close they came; he always put the lids carefully back in place. He knew the people were sleeping so he worked quietly, did everything neatly and quickly, then drove on to the next cottage.

One morning I got up, pulled my pants on, and watched him come down the road. Half-past six in the morning. When he came to my house, I said, "Hey, I just wanted to tell you what a nice job you're doing."

He didn't speak; he just looked at me and walked away. He didn't even answer.

The next week I got up and waited for him again. I watched as he loaded my trash, then I said, "You know, you do a wonderful job. I've never seen a guy tend to his work so well."

He looked at me and asked, "Hey man, are you just now coming in or already going out?" And I answered that I had gotten up to tell him he was doing a good job. He just shook his head and walked away.

I waited for him a third week because I was leaving for the rest of the summer. When he came I said, "I still want to tell you how much I appreciate what you do." And finally he lit up with a big smile.

He said, "You know something? I've been hauling garbage for twelve years. You know, in twelve years nobody has ever told me they appreciated what I was doing. My boss has never told me I do a good job. Nobody has ever said thank you!" He smiled, shook his head again as if he didn't quite believe it, and walked back to his truck.

What an example of a man who deserves respect and rarely gets it! As president of a company, I am told every day what a great job I am doing with this and that. Whether I am doing particularly well or not, I get my ego stroked and my vanity inflated. When a doctor or a professor or a politician does his job well, the praises ring in his ears. He is practically smothered with respect. But this garbage man has worked hard to do his job well for twelve years without ever a word of encouragement or thanks. And still he and millions of workers like him have it said of them by half-grown adolescents, status-conscious relatives, and new-rich neighbors, "Well, he's *just* a garbage man."

The average, ordinary, common American individual, despite his problems and his shortcomings, is worthy of respect as an individual and a productive citizen. Sure, we have problems. Sure, there is crime and welfare chiseling and dishonest dealing. Sure, there are lazy people who won't go to work and who can't be depended upon. But 80 million people went to work today! The country's plants operated today. The banks and stores were open today. All that money was handled by people who are still trustworthy and dependable. You can pick up the phone and there is someone there to get you through to the Fiji Islands or London or any place in the world. People all over the country got to work today, and were waiting there, in the restaurants and drugstores and airplanes and schools, to serve you. Some of them were sick. Some were hung over. Some had sick children. But they were there. The whole world of commerce and industry, banking, finance, hospitals, police forces, service organizations, all operated today. Think of all the alarm clocks that were set, all those who had to arrange to have gas in the tank or a bicycle by the door or to catch that old subway—that somebody else had to drive. Think of all the school buses that ran back and forth across this country in the snow or across the desert or in a driving rain.

Thousands of production lines operated today, and you'll have their goods on your table or on your kid's feet in a few weeks. You turned on the radio or TV and there was someone to tell you the time and play some music for you. People are waiting in tens of thousands of gas stations to pump gas into your car to get you where you are going.

I'm telling you—it's a fast-moving, highly efficient society we live in, and the people who work hard to keep it moving are to be saluted!

I have reflected for many years on the subject of leadership, or the qualities that make a man a good leader, and I have concluded that this thing of respect for other men is the first item on the list. If I had to train a man to take my job overnight, I would forget about trying to teach him the details of the Amway business and spend my time telling him how important it is for him to respect the people working with him and for him. Many people aspire to positions of leadership without realizing that real leadership begins with respect for people. It cannot be gained by talent, intelligence, or hard work alone. Without respect for the people one is to lead, it is impossible to be an effective leader.

Everyone wants to be chief. Not many people realize that the man who becomes a great leader and wins the respect and affection of many followers usually has a respect for his followers which is as deep and real as their respect for him.

Leadership is not something that can be conferred or granted. A man is not a leader until his people accept him as their leader. He can be their boss, their master, but he is still not their leader. A man can gain control over people by being arbitrarily placed over them, or by various authoritarian means. But leadership is more than having authority over people, more than doing the technically correct thing—it is being the person whom people want to follow. The world is filled with persons who have become managers of men, but real leaders are difficult to find. Leadership implies getting the job done through people, and that process requires mutual respect.

Somehow people know when a person respects them for what they are. People will always follow that kind of leader. Respect may be communicated in different ways, but it will invariably be communicated if it is there. In World War II the United States had two generals who were greatly different from each other: Eisenhower and Patton. Ike's image was that of a kind, gentle leader; Patton was considered harsh and demanding. But even though Patton was rough and hard-nosed, he respected the GIs under his command as competent fighting men. That respect for them, however gruffly communicated, made him a great leader. Respect for one's followers does not mean softness or lack of demands. It means a genuine faith in them as individuals who can and will get the job done. If a man knows that his leader has faith in him to do the job, he will usually do whatever is humanly possible to measure up.

My own particular "thing" has always been salesmanship. I have been involved in sales all my life, and I am always amazed to see how many people look down their noses at salesmanship as a worthy occupation. So few people have respect for salesmen that eventually the salesman has no respect for himself. He is embarrassed about what he does, intimidated by that sneering "Oh, you're *just a salesman*" stuff. As stated earlier, there are two hundred thousand independent Amway distributors working for themselves. As a leader of those people my first job is to communicate the respect that I genuinely feel, and hope that my respect will rub off on them and what they are doing. A man who believes he is just a crummy old salesman will usually act like a crummy old salesman. He will not be happy, and he will not sell very much, either.

In this day of rapid proliferation of college degrees and obsession with social status, it takes a guy who really has his head together to say simply, "I am a salesman," and not let a lack of respect from others affect him. Why? Because lots of folks think they are too good to sell. They have forgotten that every dollar that is made in America is made because somebody somewhere sold something. Sales generate all the income there is, whether it is the sale of a product or a service or whatever. I was fortunate enough to grow up in a home in which salesmanship was not looked down on, and I've never had to swallow my pride in order to sell something.

Listen to people talk about selling sometime. Their most frequent lines are, "Oh, I just hate to have to try to sell something," or "It just kills me to have to try to sell anything to someone." Do you know what the problem is? Pride. Plain and simple pride of people who hate to ask people to buy, because down deep they have no respect for the art of selling.

On top of that general disrespect for salesmanship, our Amway distributors have to combat the added contempt shown for the person-to-person salesman. I've had people say to me before, "Oh, Amway. You guys are in that direct-selling deal." My answer: Sure we are! We are in the personal-service business. We happen to think that personal service beats making the customer stand in line. We don't apologize for it. I respect the man who is in a business where the customers need not beat their way through traffic, park way out in a crowded parking lot, and run through the rain or snow to get their goods. I respect the man who brings it to their doors, and if he respects the value of his own service he is to be praised and not put down for it.

I believe it is high time for us to get off each other's backs and out of each other's hair, quit the petty sniping and fussing and bickering about this group and that group, and get on with the business of making a better life for ourselves and our children. It is time to quit tearing each other down, to quit singing, "My job is better than your job," to quit playing one-upmanship between this and that group, and start building one another up. You can try to understand my situation, look at the good in me, give me credit for a bit of intelligence and basic decency—in short, you can give me *respect*—and I will be a better person for it. And I, on the other hand, can channel the same human respect back to you, and you will be a better person for it. God wants us to get along that way, to be good for each other, to build each other up, and it all starts with respect.

When was the last time you took five minutes to say thank you in a note to that schoolteacher who wipes your kid's nose and helps him find his boots when they are lost and puts up with his racket and his rowdiness? When was the last time you thanked the policeman who gave you a speeding ticket, thanked him for his hard work with a hundred hassles every day? When was the last time a cop got that kind of respect from you? When was the last time you expressed gratitude to that usher at your church who has done his job for twenty years without complaining or shirking, for no pay and little thanks? When did you last write a note to a candidate for political office who ran and lost, just to tell him how much you respect his willingness to put it all on the line to make democracy work? How often do you tell the waitress at that restaurant where you get coffee every morning that you appreciate how hard she works every day to keep her customers happy?

Think of all those people who are your friends, your customers, clients or colleagues, those people who rub shoulders with you every day, whose hard work or friendship or special skills make your life better. How many of those people *know* how much you respect them for what they are, how much you respect the way they live their lives and do their jobs? You do respect them; you do need them and admire them in a thousand small ways. So tell them. Show them. Let that respect for them show. Turn it loose and let it show. It's what makes the world go 'round!

Believe!

...in America

Introduction

How do you feel about America's founders?
There are certainly lots of opinions out there.
Many think you should hate them. Many others think you should love them. As is usually the case in life, reality is more complicated.

The founders were human, which means they were deeply flawed. They enslaved black people. They restricted the right to vote to landowners and didn't even consider extending that right to women. None of us should overlook the founders' sins or try to excuse them.

Still, we should recognize their accomplishments and understand the tremendous progress they unleashed. They created the first country in the world founded on the promise of "Life, Liberty, and the pursuit of Happiness" for all. While they failed to live by those words, they created a country that has undeniably changed the world for the better, lifting up billions of people along the way.

How has America gotten so much right? The answer isn't just the Declaration of Independence, with its lofty language and sweeping promises. The Constitution—which came eleven years later—is just as important.

Where the Declaration laid out America's principles, the Constitution gave every generation a practical framework for applying those principles more fully. The Constitution's very first words are about forming "a more perfect Union." Ultimately, that means ending the injustices perpetuated by deeply imperfect people.

Isn't this the story of America?

For 250 years, we've struggled to realize our country's full potential, so that every American can avail themselves of their rights and fully participate in our national prosperity. It hasn't been easy. Yet the determination and work we've done to break barriers has been more than worth the effort. As we've empowered more people, we've made America the freest, wealthiest, and most successful nation in human history!

But along the way, and especially in the past fifty years, a lot of people have started thinking that all our progress springs from a poisoned seed. They say that the evils of the founding define our country. So America has been evil ever since.

The problem with this view is the lack of perspective. History is complex. So are human beings. They can advocate true principles while utterly violating those principles through their actions. We shouldn't accept those actions. But we shouldn't throw out the principles, either.

The rejection of our country's principles is an abdication of our duty as Americans. The proper response to evil is to say: Not on my watch. The generations before us stood in the breach and made America more perfect. It's up to us to continue in that tradition and make America more perfect still. If not us, who? And if not now, when?

After reading this, you may still say: Doug, you've led a privileged life. America has been good to you. But it hasn't been good to so many others. Why should I listen to you and not them?

My response is simple: Don't listen to me. Listen to Frederick Douglass.

America was not good to Frederick Douglass. He was born into slavery before the Civil War. He endured horrors that no human being should ever endure. While he escaped to freedom, he never experienced real racial equality, even as he successfully fought to end slavery once and for all. If anyone had a right to hate America, it was him.

Years later, Frederick Douglass posed a question: "What to the slave is the Fourth of July?" His answer: The Fourth of July is everything, because America is built on "saving principles."

Douglass implored his fellow Americans of all races and creeds: "Stand by those principles, be true to them on all occasions, in all places, against all foes, and at whatever cost."

If a former slave like Frederick Douglass could say those words—if he could dedicate his life to making America live by the principles espoused by the founders—surely we can do the same.

—Doug DeVos

RECENTLY A GENTLEMAN IN GRAND RAPIDS, Michigan, decided to sell his house. He called a local realtor and asked him to take the listing. The realtor returned to his office and prepared an ad to put in the paper telling about the features of this house. That evening the gentleman who had listed his house was reading the paper and looking, of course, to see if it was being advertised. He read the ad, and read it again and again. Suddenly he got up from his chair and went to the telephone. He called the realtor and told him to cancel the listing. The realtor was completely surprised and asked, "What's the matter? What caused you to suddenly change your mind? Only yesterday you wanted to sell your house and now you want me to cancel it. Why the change?"

The man's answer was very simple. He said, "After I read your ad, I suddenly realized I already live in the house I always wanted to live in."

This story is typical of many Americans who already live in a land that gives them everything they could hope for in this world, and yet they do not realize it. In the early 1950s thousands of our young men fought a war in Korea. A disturbing thing happened there which had never occurred before in the history of the United States. About seven thousand of our young men who were taken captive by the Chinese Communists sat it out. They made no attempt to escape; they just decided to take the candy and cigarettes and the food, play it cool, and not get involved. They gave up their freedom without even a contest.

A psychiatrist by the name of Meyer interviewed over a thousand of these men upon their return. His conclusion was that the young men weren't convinced that America was worth standing up for anymore.

I couldn't help but recall famous escapes of history—General MacArthur's escape from Corregidor, the hundreds of escapes by American servicemen during World War II, and the dramatic accounts from Vietnam. If the question were put to those men, "Why did you take the risk? Why did you gamble to get out of prison?" the answer would be simple. They would say, "Because we wanted to be free." And now, here were groups of Americans who weren't so sure America was worth the price.

The Communists told those boys how wonderful their system of socialism was, that it was far superior to America's capitalism and our men sat there and listened. Some believed, and many more doubted, and others weren't so sure anymore about The American Way.

I believe in America. In a time when flag-waving is discouraged, I don't apologize at all for an old-fashioned, hand-over-heart, emotional brand of patriotism. I believe that America is the greatest country in the world, with the richest past, the brightest future, and the most exciting present of any nation anywhere.

If one compares America as it is with America as it might potentially be, it is inevitable that there is plenty to fuss about. Are there problems in America? Sure there are. There is too much poverty, too much crime, too much alcoholism and divorce. There is inflation and recession and an emotional hangover still lingering from the war in Vietnam. There are plenty of problems, and only a fool would deny that they exist.

I remember when I was a kid in Sunday school the teacher always warned us not to take a Scripture verse out of its context in the Bible. When you study the Bible you take the whole chapter, the whole passage—because if you just pick a verse here and a verse there you can make the Bible prove any point you like. Too many people look at America like that. They pick a problem here and a little defect there and pretty soon they build a whole case around those few faults. They take the problems out of context and preach sermons on how America is going to the dogs!

Believe!

The worst thing about such distortion is that the people who do it are often very influential. They have an audience among the nation's young people. Our kids get all hung up on some minor defects and lose their perspective; they lose the perspective necessary to balance the debits and the credits and see the whole picture of what America is like. The only way to keep the perspective straight is to ask the second question, "Compared to what?" It is when America is compared with other countries that a true picture is most apparent. Many of us have stopped talking about the wonderful things that free enterprise has given to all of us. Let me quote a few statistics, a listing of the assets of America, and a comparison of where we stand as opposed to Communist Russia, which attempts to tell people all across the world that their system is superior to ours. It may be better for a handful of leaders, but when we look at the people who live under that system, we find them living in situations which by our standards constitute extreme poverty. Let me give you a few figures for comparison.

In order to enjoy the glories of the present Soviet system, and to bring our resources to their level, we would have to abandon half of our steel capacity, one-half of our petroleum capacity, destroy three of every five hydroelectric plants, and get along on a third of our volume of natural gas.

We would have to rip up thirteen of every fourteen miles of our paved highways, and two of every three miles of our main-line railroad tracks.

We'd scrap nineteen out of every twenty cars and trucks, destroy over two thousand colleges and universities and burn 85 percent of our museums.

We would cut our living standard by two-thirds, destroy 50 million television sets, ten out of every eleven telephones, seven of every ten single-family houses; and then we would have to put about sixty-eight million people back on the farms.

A graphic example of direct competition between the two countries was the "space race." Back in the 1950s the Russians shot the first sputnik satellite into space. We suddenly saw in headlines all across America that we had lost the space race: RUSSIA LEADS—AMERICA ISN'T EVEN CLOSE. RUSSIA WILL DOMINATE THE WORLD BY DOMINATING SPACE. Newspaper after newspaper across the world told us we were doomed because Russia had gone first into space, and we weren't even close to having anything going.

But when the American people with American ingenuity and determination put their minds to the job, we became the ones to walk on the moon. We were the ones who have been there and back. We landed a vehicle on it. Listen to the rest of the statistics: Sixteen years after the first sputnik, we had twenty-seven manned space flights compared to Russia's eighteen. We had twenty-one multiman flights compared to their nine. We had put sixty men in space, they had put thirty-two there. We had nine space walks, they had one. We had seven space linkups, they had only two. We had been to the moon four times, landed twice, and come back. They haven't put a man on it yet.

But let's forget statistics and production data for a while and talk about something much closer to the real secret of American superiority. America has always been the land of plenty—plenty of men, plenty of resources, plenty of all the necessities of life.

But when we study the history of this land we realize that it was not immigration or climate or resources alone that made America great. We see that there is another factor to be reckoned with when the American nation is judged. That factor leaves its traces in a thousand history books and millions of lives. It can be found every day of the year from Maine to Miami, from the chalets of Vermont to the ranch houses of Arizona, from the gentleman farmer of Virginia to the bartender in San Diego. This factor is the faith which binds us all together and makes of us one people. It is the spirit of America.

Believe!

The spirit of America is an intangible thing and is extremely difficult to define. It has its roots in a political philosophy, but it is more than that. One may regard it as commonly shared regional traits, but it is something more than that. It smacks strongly of nationalism and patriotism, but it goes deeper still than that.

The spirit of America is all these things lumped into one. It is the thing that sets Americans apart from all other people of the world and marks them as children of destiny. This intangible quality is expressed in the inscription on the Statue of Liberty:

> ...*Give me your tired, your poor,*
> *Your huddled masses yearning to breathe free....*

Here it is! Here is the essence of the American spirit! "...yearning to breathe free...." Yearning to taste the fullness of life, yearning to kick off restraint and plot an independent course, yearning to stretch dormant muscles and operate at full capacity, yearning to tear down old barns and build new ones, to cast off security and gamble on the long chance, to defy precedent and seek adventure.

"...yearning to breathe free...." Free to be an individual, free to be a tycoon or a gutter bum, to be everything or nothing; free to follow the inner voice, to believe or doubt, to agree or disagree; free to wear the blue or the gray, to march with Grant or with Lee.

That call of freedom went forth from a rugged wilderness, and Europe and Asia and Africa sent their sons of adventure to hew out a new society in a land of forests and savages. They came lean and hungry, tired of tyranny, eager to find new lives. And when they found that freedom of mind and body they sought, they assumed a reckless self-confidence that knew no defeat. They tore the concept of inferiority to shreds, made a shambles of the negative approach, and threw the words "second best" out of their vocabularies. Out of this came the spirit of America, and with this spirit they built our nation and forged our heritage.

...in America

Of course, there have always been those who have underestimated and discredited the power of the American spirit. One of the first of these was an English king named George. He is remembered by Britons today as the man who lost the American colonies. Another man who misjudged this spirit was a Mexican named Santa Anna. He died in poverty in Mexico City with memories of the Alamo and San Jacinto still coming back to haunt him. And then there was that man called Hitler, who scoffed at the American spirit one year and died in a Berlin bunker the next.

In this day of statistical analysis, when the "cold fact" is glorified, it is tempting to scoff and smirk when a thing such as spirit is introduced into a political problem. And now, when the United States finds itself in critical times, all the alarmists and cynics around the globe come to the conclusion that all is lost and the democratic ideals of Americanism are about to be destroyed. Of those who despair and sneer at the American spirit, history would ask a few questions:

Where were they when a handful of painted New Englanders dumped the king's tea into the briny Boston Harbor? Where were they when a thin, ragged line of angry colonists stood off the British army at Bunker Hill? Where were they when Nathan Hale flung into the face of the British army his pride in dying for his country? Where were they when the cotton bales of New Orleans spat out the fire and thunder of Andrew Jackson's fury? Where were they when brave men locked arms at the Alamo? Where were they when Johnny came marchin' home? Where were the skeptics when fever-ridden engineers scraped out the Panama Canal? Where were they when the trees of Argonne Forest shook with Yankee gunfire? Where were they when Lindbergh flew the Atlantic, when Peary crossed the North Pole, when Edison destroyed darkness with a light bulb, when Neil Armstrong kicked up dust on the moon?

The skeptics have always been there, and still America has always moved ahead, solving its problems, coping with new demands, always showing resilience and toughness when the chips were down. Sure, these are difficult times, as there have been difficult times before. But one thing can be counted on: in the crunch, the American spirit never breaks!

As a final point, I would submit to you that the real strength of America is its religious tradition. I am concerned that too many people have lost sight of the fact that America is what it is today because God has blessed this land. Too many people today are willing to act as if God had nothing whatsoever to do with it. They don't even want to mention Him anymore. This country was built on a religious heritage, and we'd better get back to it. We had better start telling people that faith in God is the real strength of America! It is true, as the Bible states, that faith comes through hearing, which demands that we begin telling of God's grace to this country.

When this country was founded, the Pilgrims offered prayer on that first Thanksgiving Day. Even to this day, as a continuation of that heritage, the United States Congress in Washington, D.C., opens with prayer at every session. Whenever I pick up a dollar bill or any piece of change I see the words "In God We Trust." This, too, is a part of that heritage, a recognition of the fact that in God is the strength of America.

We have always believed in this country that man was created in the image of God. As such he was given talents and responsibilities and was instructed to use them to make the world a better place. This is the really great thing of America, and this is what contrasts with everything that Russia and many other societies attempt to achieve. The strength of America lies in the faith of its people, who, by their efforts and their faith, have made the United States what it is.

It is time all of us began to sell America, to tell others of her assets so that they will be inspired to greater effort and renewed faith.

Perhaps the man who summed it up best was Carlos P. Romulo, soldier, statesman, and Philippine patriot, who served with General MacArthur in World War II and played a leading role in creating the

United Nations. He was the Philippine ambassador to this country for many years, and a former president of the UN General Assembly. When he left America for the last time, he said this:

I am going home, America—farewell. For seventeen years, I have enjoyed your hospitality, visited every one of your fifty states. I can say I know you well. I admire and love America. It is my second home. What I have to say now in parting is both a tribute and a warning: Never forget, Americans, that yours is a spiritual country. Yes, I know that you are a practical people. Like others, I have marveled at your factories, your skyscrapers and your arsenals. But underlying everything else is the fact that America began as a God-loving, God-fearing, God-worshiping people, knowing that there is a spark of the Divine in each one of us. It is this respect for the dignity of the human spirit which makes America invincible. May it always endure.

And so I say again in parting, thank you, America, and farewell. May God keep you always—and may you always keep God.

Believe!, first published in 1975, was the first book Rich DeVos wrote. It always held a special place in his heart. In the 1980s, the book served as the inspiration for a full length feature film by the same title.

At right: Believe! *movie poster.*

Below: *Rich DeVos posing with the* Believe! *book for promotional materials.*

As referenced in Introduction, page xiv.

Rich DeVos, a passionate champion of American principles, shared close friendships with Presidents Ronald Reagan and Gerald R. Ford. They were bound by their mutual love of freedom, faith, and the enduring promise of the American Dream.

At top: *Rich DeVos bonding with President Ford on the golf course.*
Below: *Betty Ford, President Ronald Reagan, and Rich DeVos.*

As referenced in Introduction, page xvi.

October 3, 1974

Dear Helen and Rich:

I can't tell you how glad I was to see you both
again and to receive your note afterwards. Old
friends have a wonderful way of renewing the
spirit. So many years spent working with you
in Michigan and for you in Washington have
built up personal ties that can never be replaced.

I wholeheartedly agree with you, Rich, that there
is truly a great deal right with America. We do
need to talk positively about the strengths of
America and about the unfailing ability and genius
of our people to resolve problems and make real
progress.

Again, I want you both to know how good it was to
see you. I sincerely appreciate your continuing
deep concern and staunch support.

With warmest personal regards,

Sincerely,

Jerry Ford

Mr. and Mrs. Richard M. DeVos
7154 Windy Hill Road, S. E.
Grand Rapids, Michigan 49506

**Over their decades-long friendship, President Gerald R. Ford often sent
Rich DeVos personal letters—warm, handwritten notes reflecting their deep
mutual respect, shared values, and unwavering belief in America's ideals.**

Above: *A letter from President Ford to Rich DeVos.*
Shown opposite: *Handwritten letters from President Ford to Rich DeVos.*

As referenced in Introduction, page xvi.

GERALD R. FORD   March 3rd

Dear Rich;

Thanks for the
video - Compassionate Capitalism,
which I look forward to seeing.

I deeply appreciate your
many kindnesses + friendship.
It has been wonderful to work
with you for so many, many
years.

Betty + I wish Helen + you our
very best.   Jerry Ford

LOG YACHT

From			To				Date	
STAR PRINTING CO., BOSTON								
Time	Log	Chart Course	Course Steered	Wind	Bar.	Ther.	REMARKS	
2000							WATER ON DECK IN CABIN. TURN BILGE PUMP ON.	
2005							GETTING DEEPER ONE MAN STARTS PUMPING. GAINING ON IT NOW, SO WE PROCEED ON COURSE.	
2100							LEAKING FASTER. ONE MAN PUMPING CAN NOT KEEP UP WITH IT. GET OUT ANOTHER BILGE PUMP.	
2200							BARELY KEEPING EVEN NOW. HOPE TO MAKE CAY LOBOS LIGHT	
24:00							LOSING BIT BY BIT NOW. CAN NOT KEEP UP WITH IT	
TUES. MARCH 19							GIVING DISTRESS OVER RADIO.	
00:15							SIGHT SHIP N.E. OF US. SEND UP DISTRESS SIGNALS. HE BLINKS BACK TO US. WE GAVE HIM AN SOS.	
00:45							SHIP IGNORES US & CONTINUES ON VOYAGE	

LOG YACHT

From			To				Date	
STAR PRINTING CO., BOSTON								
Time	Log	Chart Course	Course Steered	Wind	Bar.	Ther.	REMARKS	
0100							SIGHT ANOTHER SHIP ON HORIZON.	
1:54							SENT UP DISTRESS FLARES.	
2:00							SHIPS TURNS & COMES TOWARD US.	
2:38							APABELLE LYKES COMES ALONGSIDE & WE SECURE THERE WE REMOVE OUR PERSONAL GEAR & ABANDON SHIP. CAPT. W.H FILES, SKIPPER OF TH APABELLE LYKES. SENT HIS MEN ON THE SHIP IN AN EFFORT TO SAVE HER. THEY WORKED TIL 5:00 AM. & FINALLY GAVE IT UP AS IMPOSSIBLE AT 5:30 AM. SHE SANK.	

FINI

Richard De Vos
Jay Van Andel
Eugene Hernandez

Above: *Final entries from the Elizabeth logbook.*
Left: *The original Elizabeth logbook.*

Before building a business empire, Rich DeVos and Jay Van Andel tried sailing to South America—and sank off Cuba. Their first venture? A leaky schooner named Elizabeth and a dream that nearly drowned.

As referenced in Believe in... Unlimited Potential, page 8.

Photo of the Elizabeth.

Right: *A sculpture at Amway's World Headquarters that now displays the Ten Pillars of Economic Wisdom.*

Below: *The Hall of Free Enterprise at the 1964 World's Fair.*

As referenced in Believe in... Free Enterprise; page 37.

The Ten Pillars of Economic Wisdom—originally displayed at the 1964 World's Fair—now stand outside Amway's World Headquarters, a lasting tribute to Rich and Jay's deep belief in people and the power of free enterprise.

For Rich DeVos, family was the anchor of his life—and sailing, a lifelong passion that became both a bonding tradition and a powerful metaphor for navigating challenges, charting purpose, and staying steady through life's unpredictable winds.

Above: *Rich DeVos and wife Helen DeVos, and their four children, Dick, Dan, Cheri, and Doug.*

As referenced in Believe in... Family; page 107.

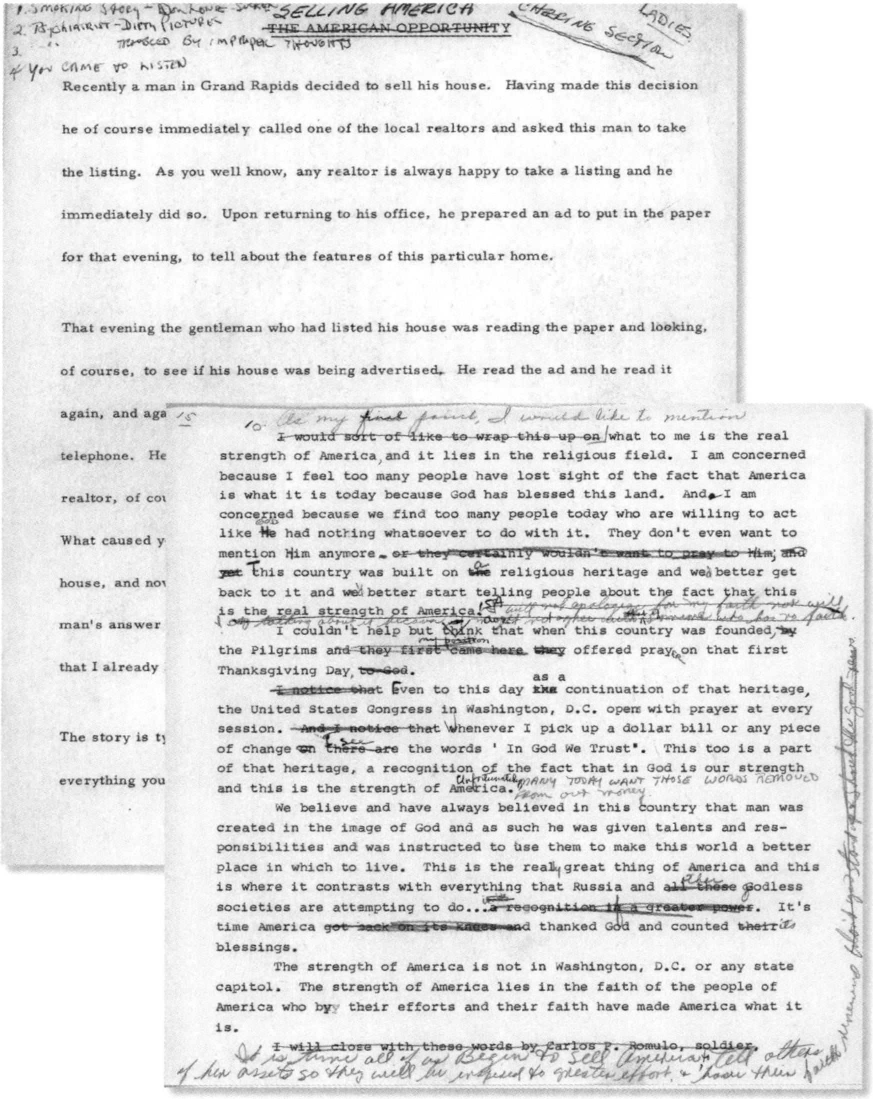

Handwritten header notes:
1. SMOKING STORY — DON LOVE SURE SELLING AMERICA
2. PSYCHIATRIST — DIRTY PICTURES — THE AMERICAN OPPORTUNITY
3. ... TROUBLED BY IMPROPER THOUGHTS
4. YOU CAME TO LISTEN

CHECKING SECTION LADIES

Recently a man in Grand Rapids decided to sell his house. Having made this decision

he of course immediately called one of the local realtors and asked this man to take

the listing. As you well know, any realtor is always happy to take a listing and he

immediately did so. Upon returning to his office, he prepared an ad to put in the paper

for that evening, to tell about the features of this particular home.

That evening the gentleman who had listed his house was reading the paper and looking,

of course, to see if his house was being advertised. He read the ad and he read it

again, and aga...

telephone. He...

realtor, of cou...

What caused y...

house, and nov...

man's answer...

that I already...

The story is t...

everything you...

As my final point, I would like to mention

I would sort of like to wrap this up on what to me is the real
strength of America and it lies in the religious field. I am concerned
because I feel too many people have lost sight of the fact that America
is what it is today because God has blessed this land. And I am
concerned because we find too many people today who are willing to act
like He had nothing whatsoever to do with it. They don't even want to
mention Him anymore or they certainly wouldn't want to pray to Him, and
yet this country was built on the religious heritage and we better get
back to it and we better start telling people about the fact that this
is the real strength of America.

I couldn't help but think that when this country was founded by
the Pilgrims and they first came here they offered pray on that first
Thanksgiving Day, to God.

I notice that Even to this day the continuation of that heritage,
the United States Congress in Washington, D.C. opens with prayer at every
session. And I notice that whenever I pick up a dollar bill or any piece
of change on there are the words ' In God We Trust'. This too is a part
of that heritage, a recognition of the fact that in God is our strength
and this is the strength of America.

We believe and have always believed in this country that man was
created in the image of God and as such he was given talents and responsibilities and was instructed to use them to make this world a better
place in which to live. This is the real great thing of America and this
is where it contrasts with everything that Russia and all these godless
societies are attempting to do... a recognition is a greater power. It's
time America got back on its knees and thanked God and counted their
blessings.

The strength of America is not in Washington, D.C. or any state
capitol. The strength of America lies in the faith of the people of
America who by their efforts and their faith have made America what it
is.

I will close with these words by Carlos P. Romulo, soldier,...

Rich DeVos's original handwritten notes—worn at the edges and marked with edits—reveal how tirelessly he refined his iconic "Selling America" speech, driven by a deep conviction to inspire belief in the American Dream.

Above: *Rich DeVos' handwritten edits to "Selling America" speech.*

Opposite top: *Selling America vinyl LP cover.* Below: *Selling America speech notecards.*

As referenced in *Selling America*, page 117.

Italian + Polish = Topless + Bottomless

Selling America

"SELLING ⚒ AMERICA"

RICHARD DE VOS

2.
It is time to talk about our common interests, not our differences.
        Lives are changed by the LITTLE DECISIONS we make.
1. A thank you note
2. A visit to a sick friend
3. Ladies dresses or hats
4. Lonely kid in school
5. You can do it to co-worker or fellow student
6. Looking yellow
Yes, you can change lives. Begin to look for good.
1. School bus drivers
2. Janitors
3. Mechanics
4. Employment – 80 million
5. Teachers

JET
COFFEE
8 + 9 K work

7.
12. RELIGION _ Real strength.
    a. Great because of faith
    b. Belief in each other
    c. Spirit of God in man
    d. "In God We Trust"
    e. People build – not Gov't.
    f. 700 Churches in Moscow - now 5

I will close with these words by Carlos P. Romulo, soldier, statesman and Phillippine patriot, who served with General MacArthur in World War II and played a leading role in creating the United Nations; a former Pres. of the UN General Assembly, and ambassador to this country for many years. When he returned, he said this:

"I am going home, America - farewell. (8)
For 17 years, I have enjoyed your hospitality, visited every one of your 50 states. I can say I know you well. I admire and love America. It is my second home. What I have to say now in parting is both a tribute & a warning: Never forget, Americans, that yours is a spiritual country. Yes, I know that you are a practical people. Like others, I have marveled at your factories, your skyscrapers & your arsenals. But underlying everything else is the fact that America began as a God-loving, God-fearing, God-worshipping people, knowing that there is a spark of the Divine in each one of us. It is this respect for the dignity of the human spirit which makes America invincible. May it always endure. And so I say again in parting, thank you, America, & farewell. May God keep you always - & may you always keep God."

Believe!

...in the Power of Persistence

Introduction

Here's one of the most shocking things I've read in recent years. One in three Americans is *afraid* of failure. Not only that, more Americans fear failure than they do spiders, being home alone, and even the paranormal!

To be clear, I don't like failure. (Or spiders.) I don't know anyone who does. But not liking failure is a lot different than fearing failure.

When you're afraid of failure, you're more likely to give up when things go wrong. Why run the risk of falling short again?

Worse, you're a lot less likely to put yourself in positions where you could fail at all. Why try in the first place?

But you know what happens if you don't try, or if you give up too soon? Things don't get better. Those barriers are still there. You've just stopped trying to break free.

By barriers, I mean literally anything that holds us back. Maybe it's your income—you need a raise. Maybe it's a misunderstanding in your marriage—you're talking past each other. Moving forward may not be easy. But if you never try, you'll never get there.

I often think of Thomas Edison, who broke the barrier of darkness by creating the light bulb. He famously tried many failed experiments. When a friend asked him about his lack of results, he yelled: "I have gotten lots of results! I know several thousand things that won't work!"

This is the classic American ethos—the total determination to never stop trying in search of success. But as the fear of failure has risen, so has our hunger to make a difference. Fewer people are starting small businesses. Fewer people are pursuing their dreams. Heck, fewer young men are asking out young women. They fear rejection. Shouldn't they fear loneliness more?

This fear of failure, and resulting unwillingness to even try, only makes things worse. You'll miss untold opportunities and experiences. You'll never be able to reach your full potential.

And what's true for individuals is true for our country.

It feels like it's getting harder to do big things or dream big dreams anymore. Instead, institutions like the government are trying to guarantee outcomes and take the risk out of life. Yet Americans are also increasingly unhappy with our country's direction.

Well, how are we going to do better if we don't try something new? Are we really going to let the fear of failure prevent us from pursuing the possibility of success?

Remember that success takes many forms and builds on itself. Before you make a million dollars, you have to make a thousand dollars. Before you build a big business, you have to start a small business. And before you win the race, you have to make it out of the starting block.

I say this as someone who has experienced failure many times.

Case in point: Our family owns the Orlando Magic. They've made it to the NBA Finals twice but didn't win. I'm a Purdue alum, and the Boilermakers were in the 2024 men's basketball finals but didn't win. And my beloved Detroit Lions...well...let's just move on.

Perhaps the most famous example of my failure was in the 36th America's Cup in 2021.

I'd helped put together a sailing team called American Magic. We partnered with the New York Yacht Club to participate in the cup, which was first sailed in 1851. It's the most prestigious event in sailing, and the oldest event in all of the sport.

Believe!

As we entered the competition, we truly believed we could win. But in one of the qualifying races, disaster struck. We were winning the race against Italy and all we had to do was round the final mark and sail to the finish. As we turned to the home stretch, a gust of wind hit us hard. The boat flew out of the water, landed hard, and capsized. Once we accounted for the safety of the crew, we realized we had a hole in the hull. The boat was sinking. We had to act fast.

Thankfully, we saved the boat before it went completely under. (While I don't like to relive it, you can find several videos online.) But our chance of winning was gone. Still, we didn't give up. The team miraculously repaired the boat in just over a week and we jumped back into the competition. We didn't win, but we sure didn't quit. And we'll never win if we don't keep persevering.

What about you? Fear stops you from even showing up to play the game—whatever game it is. And if you never try, you can never succeed. What we need today is for every American to play their heart out.

—*Doug DeVos*

WHEN OUR CHILDREN WERE SMALL, we often read them the story of *The Little Engine That Could.* Over the years, thousands of young people have heard this story and caught its message: There is no substitute for a determined belief that hard work and effort will always pay off.

If I had to select one quality, one personal characteristic that I regard as being most highly correlated with success, whatever the field, I would pick the trait of persistence. Determination. The will to endure to the end, to get knocked down seventy times and get up off the floor saying, "Here goes number seventy-one!"

Of course, some people confuse persistence with stubbornness. They think determination and mule-headedness are one and the same. They are not. One can be foolishly and nonproductively stubborn. He can be stubborn about almost anything from insisting that water is not wet to demanding that time stand still. Stubbornness often exists for its own sake, with no relationship to reality or function. Persistence, on the other hand, is stubbornness with a purpose. It is determination with a goal in mind. One dictionary defines persistence as "a tenacious will to exist, a hardy struggle against odds."

The thing that elevates persistence above the level of stubbornness is that persistence flows from a decision that has been made toward a goal that is in sight. Random, aimless stubbornness is an annoying quality, but persistence that follows a decision in an individual's life can be the single most important characteristic in his chances of success or failure.

I had an experience early in my high-school days that taught me the value of making tough decisions and persisting in them. My first year in high school I attended Grand Rapids Christian High School, a private school. I really didn't think a lot about the fact that I was going to a private school, or that it was costing my dad lots of hard-earned money. I was just there. So I chased the girls and I goofed off. I was not the best student in the world, so I'm the kind of person who has to apply, and I didn't apply! I didn't actually flunk anything, although the only way I scraped through Latin was by promising never to take it again.

My dad was pretty unhappy about my poor grades that first year, so he said, "Well, son, if that's the way it's going to be, if you're going to goof off anyway, I'm not going to pay this money to send you to private school." So the next year I went to a public school. I didn't like it there, and when my third year of high school rolled around, I told Dad that I intended to go back to Christian High School. "Humph," he said, "if you go back there I hope you realize that you are going to have to pay for it yourself." That really laid it on the line. I could stay at the public school, or I could switch back to Christian High. The decision was mine to make. But if I went to the school that I preferred, I was going to have to be determined enough to pay the freight. I thought it over. I figured out the cost. I had a job at a gas station, and I thought I could make enough money to pay the tuition as I went, so I said, "I'm going back to Christian High School. I'll pay the bill myself."

That was the first time in my life I had ever made a decision of that magnitude, a decision that had to be followed up, that had to be backed up by persistence and determination. I look back on that autumn day as an important time in my growth. It was a point in my life where, for the first time, I not only decided to do something which I chose to do, but I was willing to back it up by saying, "This is the price I'll pay to get it." (To finish that story, my parents eventually helped with my tuition, after seeing that I was serious in my choice.)

It takes a decision to turn persistence loose and let it operate. Some people will never know whether they have any real capacity for determination, because they will never put themselves on the line and commit themselves to a decision that they know might require sleepless nights and long, hard days of work.

It is amazing how much of our lives is determined not by big decisions, but by little ones that pile up on us until the big ones are automatically made. The average person usually says that the biggest decision he ever made was the day he decided to get married. I've had a lot of men tell me that, and I laugh, because I have never met a fellow yet who decided to get married. What happened, you see, was that he made a little decision to ask a certain girl out. And then he tried it again. And things just gradually moved on from there and the next thing he knew he was married and had a family and he had a job and so on. Another "big" decision is the job a man works at. But usually he didn't make any kind of major decision. It just happened to be a handy thing at the time it came up, and the firm had an opening, and so he took it and he couldn't afford to quit and on he goes.

It takes real courage to make a major decision; to really take a look at one's situation and dare to grab things by the throat and make a tough, important decision. But that is the only way to get on the track toward goals that really matter. Ben Jonson, one of the great English writers, once said, "What is written without effort is generally read without pleasure." That is the way it is with decisions. Very often those things that are decided without pain and commitment, without counting the cost and taking a risk, are generally pursued without passion or persistence. Life just rocks along, and things stay pretty much the same as they have always been.

Once you select a goal that is really important to you and make a decision to pursue it, the next step is to make up your mind before you set out toward it that it is going to require lots of hard work. You know that and you accept it. You make up your mind before you start that sacrifice is part of the package. In the Amway business we tell thousands of people every year about the opportunity to get ahead by developing a second career in direct selling. But we never try to make it sound easy. If a guy is looking for a shortcut to prosperity, we don't want him. When you set out to get that promotion, or to earn that degree, or to build that vacation house, or to learn that new skill, you may as well know that an eight-hour day won't be good enough anymore. If you are afraid to work more than eight hours, don't even start out to improve your situation. If you are a nut about television and you just *must* watch it, then forget about that extra goal. If bowling is the center of your life and you just can't give up three nights a week at the neighborhood lanes, then go ahead and resign yourself to stay pretty much where you are in life.

If all these things are important to you, that's fine. There is nothing wrong with those things. But if you are so hooked on them that you are never going to go after those things you've always talked about, then at least stop complaining and envying the other fellow, and try to enjoy what you have. Go ahead and do all the things that fill up your time and that never force you to push yourself and improve yourself. But don't cry because other people have more than you have.

When you find a goal and have the commitment to work for it even when you feel like taking it easy, then all that is left is to persist! Keep on keeping on. Take the peaks and the valleys in stride and roll on toward that goal. Don't let the odds that are against you or the obstacles that fall in your path dissuade you for a moment. Persist. That is the key. Get your eyes so firmly on the goal that you don't have time to listen to all the reasons that you can't make it.

One of the most inspiring stories I have ever heard was the account of how a man named Robert Manry took a 13½-foot boat and sailed it across the Atlantic Ocean. If he had asked me before he left, I would have told him to stay home. There was no way he could make it. But fortunately, he didn't ask me. He fell overboard six times; he had to tie himself to the mast to keep from being washed away in storms, but he made it. He got across safely and became quite famous in sailing circles for it.

The experiences Jay Van Andel and I had in the first few years of the Amway Corporation remind me somewhat of that sailor. If we had listened to anyone, we would never have begun. We are often asked if we visualized a company of the present size from the outset. The answer is an emphatic *no!* Neither of us ever had a master plan, a grand scheme, a dream of a quarter-billion-dollar-sales-per-year company.

I'll never forget the night we decided to have a go at it. We were students at Calvin College at the time, and we were in Florida together for the Christmas vacation. We were lying in a bed in a little house in Florida, bursting with ideas for getting started in business. So we made the decision that night: Let's quit talking about it and *do* it! Let's go on with it! Let's just *charge!*

We had a simple goal: to build a successful business for ourselves. We were prepared to make whatever sacrifices were necessary to meet that goal. And we persisted. When we passed one point, only then did we look ahead to the next one. When we had the first million dollars in gross sales, then we thought about the second million. When we outgrew the first building we built another one. And gradually we saw what is now the international Amway Corporation develop. Persistence—not brilliant planning or blind luck or clever promotion—has been the key.

I remember one night in Lansing, Michigan, Jay and I had a big sales meeting. That was in the early days. It was really going to be a dandy meeting! We had been on radio with big ads, had put notices in the papers. All day long we collared people and passed out brochures, revving up for the big meeting. We had an auditorium with two hundred seats, and that night two people showed up! Did you ever make a rock-'em-sock-'em sales speech to two people in a room with two hundred seats in it? And then drive home at two o'clock in the morning because you couldn't afford to pay those motel rates? In situations like that, night after night, you do one of two things. Either you give up, or you persist. We persisted.

We started the business in our basements, but one thing led to another, and we recruited more and more people to sell our two products. So we bought a garage. Not a big place—just a sixty-by-forty-foot space. We bought two acres and almost passed up a chance to buy two more because we thought we would never need it. We decided to get it anyway, thinking we could use it for a parking lot. Things just grew and grew. We tried everything that caught our fancy. If it worked we made it a part of our product line. If it didn't, we discarded it. Trial and error. We tried selling fallout shelters, until we discovered how much fun it was to dig a hole and bury one of those things in the ground! We sold battery additives, and the batteries froze. We sold electric generators. We even sold water softeners for a while. I remember clearly the night that we decided against staying with the water-softener business. A woman called me at two o'clock in the morning to tell me her water softener was making a funny noise! We learned the hard way!

If I could wish for any person in the United States a single quality to secure for him success in life, I would not grant to him a massive intellect or a well-coordinated, athletic body. I would not wish for him glibness of tongue or personal popularity. I would not bless him with physical attractiveness or talent. I would wish for him the ability and the will to persist toward whatever his goal.

I enjoy sailing. There are many lessons to be learned on the water, and one of them is that there is no such thing as a bad wind. All winds are good winds if one knows what to do with them. Any breeze will take a sailing ship to its destination if it is properly handled. In life, when the foul winds blow, that is a lesson to remember. A few lines of verse by Ella Wheeler Wilcox make the point:

One ship drives east another drives west With the selfsame
 winds that blow.
'Tis the set of sails And not the gales
Which tells us the way to go.

Like the winds of the sea are the winds of fate, As we voyage
 along through life,
'Tis the set of the soul That decides its goal
And not the calm or the strife.

Believe!

...in God and His Church

Introduction

Faith is everything to me. I believe in Jesus Christ as my personal Savior. While many people are uncomfortable talking about their faith—and while many others think religion has no place in the public square—I'm not ashamed of it. In fact, as a Christian, I want more people to believe in Jesus, who loves you more than you can ever imagine.

But I also recognize that your faith journey may be different. You may pray in a different way. You may believe in a different god. You may believe in no god at all. Without question, America has more religions—and more people with no religion—than ever before. It's creating friction that didn't used to exist. And as religion has fallen out of favor, a lot of people have made politics into a kind of faith.

The danger is that these differences will divide us to the point of breaking. There are already plenty of warning signs. In times like these, we need grace.

In Christianity, grace is God's outpouring of love for humanity. He offers us the gift of eternal life in heaven with Him—not because we are good, but because God is good.

But here on Earth, grace has another meaning. It's about giving each other the benefit of the doubt and forgiving each other when we make mistakes. It's about showing generosity, not judgment. It's also about showing curiosity and respect for what others believe.

Believe!

Sure, their beliefs are different from yours, but learning about them helps you understand who they really are. For some reason, we've stopped trying to understand each other.

A few months before I wrote this, I hosted a big meeting of community, business, and faith leaders in my hometown of Grand Rapids. We were there to talk about some pretty tough topics. Poverty. Economic exclusion. The legacy of racism. You know, the kind of topics that get people pretty worked up.

I kicked the meeting off. From the start, I acknowledged that we had some hard discussions ahead of us. I also acknowledged that I might use some words or phrases that others don't like. Not because I wanted to hurt anyone, but because I genuinely don't know how to talk about some of these things. I ended by simply asking everyone to give me a little grace if I were to say something that troubled them.

Those words set the tone for the entire day. We pushed through the tough discussions to begin a shared search for solutions to our city's problems. We looked beyond our differences, finding common ground in some unexpected places. Things could have gotten heated, but they stayed cool, precisely because we all showed each other grace.

Sadly, in my experience, showing grace can be a rarity in America today.

All too often, we fly off the handle when we hear something we don't like. We judge people far more harshly than we judge ourselves. We write off people who disagree with us, thinking to ourselves: Could anything good come from talking to them? Isn't it better to ignore or attack them since, in all likelihood, they're going to ignore or attack me?

Admittedly, this is a very human reaction. But grace summons our better angels while helping us see the humanity in others.

To be clear, grace doesn't mean watering down your own beliefs. It doesn't mean compromising on the things you value most. Grace is not an apology for standing strong in your convictions.

But grace does mean listening to—and respecting—other people's strong convictions. It means accepting them for who they are, imperfections and all. And yes, grace means acknowledging that you're not perfect, either. We all make mistakes. We all want to be forgiven when we do. If that's going to happen, we need to extend that same courtesy—that same grace—to others.

America is an amazing melting pot of people from all sorts of backgrounds and beliefs. Given this fact, we'll always have some level of division. And yet, amid our differences, we can still find plenty of areas to unite. If we're going to find common ground again, maybe the place to start is by showing each other a little grace.

—*Doug DeVos*

As strongly as I believe in free enterprise, human dignity, accountability, an optimistic outlook, and the other principles already discussed there is one thing in which I believe even more strongly.

I believe in a personal God, in His Son Jesus Christ, and in the mission of His church.

Admittedly, a man's view of God is an extremely personal matter. And his relationship with God is perhaps the most intimate thing in his entire life. I have never been one to intrude my own personal religious convictions into the lives of other persons against their will. Ultimately, however, a man must be willing to declare publicly the faith which he feels in his heart. Without being dogmatic or pushy, he must be willing to share, with whomever will listen, the convictions which he has found important in his own life.

Occasionally people ask me, "Is Amway a Christian organization?" I always answer that it certainly is not. It has lots of wonderful Christian people in it, but an organization cannot be Christian. Only people can be Christian, because Christianity is a person-to-Person thing. It is a one-to-One relationship between an individual and Jesus Christ. I refuse to use the machinery of the Amway Corporation to foist my private convictions on others, and conversely, I do not use the Gospel to promote my business. But I cannot compartmentalize the person I am. I cannot hang my religion on the hat rack as I leave the church on Sunday and pick it up again when I return a week later. I am a Christian by faith and by experience, and in no aspect of my life can I make major decisions or take positions which are not compatible with my discipleship.

I cannot remember a time when I did not believe in God. I had the good fortune of growing up in a Christian family, and I've known the feel of the church pew from my earliest recollection. In high school I began to notice that there was a difference between the company of Christian people and those who had no faith. I was not very analytical at the time, but I knew the general atmosphere among Christians was somehow different. There was a greater warmth, a surer sense of meaning and purpose, more deeply felt interpersonal bonds among those who shared a common Christian faith. I became aware that there were two kinds of people in the world: those who loved God and embraced His church, and those who did not. And I knew that it was with the Christian group that I belonged.

Soon after returning from military service in World War II, I joined the Christian Reformed Church, and I have been a member since that time. But only in the last few years have I really known the excitement and blessing that comes from being a totally involved Christian. For many years I was a fairly typical church member going to worship services, paying my fair share of the church's support, but never making my discipleship a major part of my life. In the last few years, my wife and I have "moved off dead center," to use her words, and it has been an exciting experience to follow God's lead as He has helped us to grow up in Him.

Somehow people seem surprised to hear a corporation president discuss the importance of spiritual things. The stereotype is that the big-business executive is ruthless and mercenary, concerned only with the bottom line, far too preoccupied with material things to care about the things of the Spirit. I cannot imagine a more inaccurate image. There is nothing that can convince a man of the inadequacy of money quite so fast as having some of it! A poor man might go a lifetime with the delusion that if he only had enough money all his problems would disappear. When he acquires a fortune, he discovers just how limited money can be. Money cannot buy peace of mind. It cannot heal ruptured relationships, or build meaning into a life that has none. It cannot relieve guilt or speak to the great agonies of the broken heart.

No one knows this better than the man with money. If he is honest with himself, he knows that all that he has materially comes from the hand of God, and only in combination with worship of that God can his money bring real happiness.

At the same time, material things are not to be automatically regarded as antispiritual. Many people holler about the evils of materialism as if material things were somehow intrinsically bad. That is an illogical attitude. It makes absolutely no sense to me to make materialism the scapegoat for man's lack of interest in spiritual things. Everything in the world is material. The Bible is material— black ink on paper with leather binding. A minister wears a suit made of material, preaches from a pulpit made of material, through a microphone made of material. Obviously there is nothing wrong with material—out of it God created all things. It is only the excessive love of material things that Scripture condemns.

I believe that material goods were put on this earth for people to enjoy. God does not object to that. The Bible tells us not to worship material things, of course, but it does not tell us not to enjoy the fruits of the earth and man's labor. It is significant that God thought it important to restore to Job all his material wealth after Satan had taken it away. Job was faithful to God, and God apparently wanted him to enjoy not only spiritual blessings but material wealth as well as a reward for that faithfulness. God obviously does not regard material wealth as evil in and of itself.

That is not to say that the pursuit of money may not be a problem for a Christian. Without doubt, a man's money can come between him and God. Money is power. It brings to a man the power to make his day-to-day routine less difficult, to move other men this way or that, to exercise greater control over the conditions under which he lives. And that power can corrupt. If he becomes intoxicated with the power which money brings and forgets that the source of his money is the hand of God, then he becomes arrogantly self-reliant, forgetting that God owns all things, and gives or withholds them at His pleasure. The most effective way for a man to keep his material blessings in true perspective is to remind himself constantly that all of it comes from God.

Sometimes I think about the many people who are smarter, more deserving, more talented than I am, and I ask God, *"Why, Lord, have things worked out this way for me? Why me and not someone else?"* I think of the innumerable little miracles beyond my control which have worked together so beautifully to my benefit, and I can only acknowledge that all I have is truly God's, and for some reason I am His steward over it.

The primary thing is to maintain a sense of dependence on God. That is what humility is all about. But God is as much interested in the attitude of a $150-a-week man toward his money as he is with a millionaire's attitude. The wealthy man has more to account for, more responsibility for the way he uses his surplus, but God is still interested in the state of his heart more than in the shape of his net-worth statement. When He blesses a man materially, He does it for a reason greater than merely that individual's personal comfort, and the man with money must accept accountability for that higher purpose. He can never escape God's requirement that he answer for his use of what he has.

I would not be honest if I didn't admit that on occasions I feel a tinge of guilt for the standard of living that we enjoy here in America. Maybe the word "uneasy" is a better choice. But I don't think there is anything unusual about that. I think that every middle-class American, if he is candid, will admit that he is made uncomfortable when he thinks about the starving children in Biafra, the 200 million people in India who live on less than forty dollars a year, the poverty in Bangladesh, the great needs of people in our own country. Certainly all of us who live in nice homes, drive comfortable automobiles, and eat three square meals a day must feel a bit uneasy when we are confronted with the poverty of much of the world.

But we must remember that a poor man cannot help another poor man. An impoverished nation cannot help another impoverished nation get on its feet. There has always been poverty in the world, and it does not help the situation for men—or nations—of material strength to wallow in some kind of neurotic guilt about that fact. Like any person who has a high standard of living—which includes almost every person reading this book—I can only thank God for His help and vow to be a responsible, generous steward of what I have. In a famous parable that Christ told, a man gave one of his servants five pieces of money, and to another servant He gave only one. He did not demand of the man who was given the five that he redistribute his wealth. He did not want that man to give his five talents to those who had only two or one. Instead he demanded that the man given more money should keep it, use it, enlarge it, and make more with it. The servant that was given one talent sinned by being stingy with what he had been given, and in being afraid to work with it—perhaps even risk it—to make more of it (*see* Matthew 25).

Apart from the problems of greed and arrogance, the other evil associated with money is the sin which occurs when money is gained unfairly, at the expense of others. God does not want any man to be wealthy so much that He would approve of his taking advantage of others. Industry had a bad record on that score in the last century and the first half of the 1900s. No question about it—there were many abuses of the working man, and of the consumer, by certain industries and businesses in the past. I don't want to be overly defensive of big business, or take a naïve, Pollyanna position, but I believe that such abuses are rare today. A great majority of businessmen or industrialists genuinely want to deliver the best product they can at the lowest price, and they want happy employees who are well paid for their work. I cannot buy the image of the big-business leader as a hard-nosed, hard-hearted, rip'-em-off Scrooge who cruelly builds a fortune at the expense of the worker and the public. Over the long haul, businessmen who operate on the basis of greed and manipulation are not successful. Somewhere along the way most of them are done in by their own dishonesty and scheming. There are exceptions, of course, but I still believe that there is a certain justice in the world which rewards goodness and punishes badness.

Can a sensitive young man get to the top of the business world without compromising his Christian commitment? Of course he can! If he remembers that he is responsible to God for both his money and his relationships with other people, he can go to the very top in business without losing an ounce of his love for God or his commitment to Christian brotherhood. And if he does, he can make as great a contribution to the Kingdom of God through his business skills as any minister can do through his theological training or any missionary can do with his medical skills.

After all, can you imagine how the church would do its work without the thousands of committed businessmen who support its programs? Can you imagine a church with nothing but ministers in it? Impossible! And make no mistake about it: the church and its work are important. With all its shortcomings and critics, the church is still a vital institution to the Kingdom of God and to this nation; and for it to do its job, it needs the support of millions of hardworking, turned-on Christians.

The claim that the church is dead and lifeless is not without basis in many cases. There are thousands of congregations which have long ago lost their "first love," abandoned the task of spreading the Gospel and winning new converts, and have become social clubs whose members are going through the motions, primarily for the sake of tradition—and a vague sense that it is the right thing to do. I can understand that, because for many years my wife and I fit that description pretty closely. Our faith was not a personal thing with us; we were not emotionally involved; we were unconcerned about converting the lost and reaching new people with the message of Christ.

And that is where many church members in churches of every faith are today.

When those kinds of members fill the pews, the church drifts off on tangents that have little to do with spreading the Gospel. The primary business of the church is not to develop welfare projects, lead in political activism, quibble endlessly over tiny theological issues, and all the other quasi-religious activities with which it gets involved. The work of the church is to tell the Gospel as effectively as possible to as many people as possible. There is nothing wrong with social involvement; it is just not the most important aspect of the church's work. The church has limited resources. It simply cannot solve all the social ills of the world. And so often it becomes so absorbed in that area that it ignores its real purpose. It gets so bogged down in the training sessions and the reaction programs, the dividing of the resources to this program and that program, the quibbling over who will chair what committee, that it gets totally off the track of bringing new people to the Lord.

When the church changes from an organization concerned with evangelism to one which is preoccupied with internal, irrelevant squabbles and "busywork," it follows a pattern often seen in other institutions. I have watched the changes in various institutions for years—churches, companies, homes, even the nation itself—and have seen the same evolution occur over and over. An institution, if it doesn't constantly resist it, inevitably and gradually follows this vitality-draining pattern. There are four stages in the course of these changes: (1) the creating stage; (2) the organizing stage; (3) the defending stage; (4) the stage of "dividing the spoils."

In the *first* stage, someone starts out with a dream, an idea, a burning motivation. It could be a young family setting out to make a good life for itself, a church being organized by a group of new Christians, a business or company with a unique idea, or even a nation newly carved from some older political system. In any case, it is an exciting venture, a challenging time of building something from nothing. It is the creative stage, the building stage, when all the energies of all the people are constantly poured into making the organization a bigger and better one.

The *second* stage is the time when growth is coming, progress is occurring, and the people of the institution divert time and energy from the building and creating function and devote it to organizing and managing what has been created. There is nothing particularly wrong with this. It is all necessary and important work. Offices must be decorated; staff must be hired; buildings must be built; policies must be elaborated; in short, the growing organization must be cared for. The problem is that this managerial work is usually done by the people who formerly were on the front end of the group, the building end. Now the work of creating new customers for the business—or new members for the church or new demand for the product—is done by staff members. It is subcontracted out, since the leadership of the group is very busy managing what has already been developed.

Stage *three* is the time when the primary concern becomes defending the acquisitions of the group from outside competition or encroachment. One business begins knocking its competitors, or seeking advantages against them. The organization becomes obsessed with safety, with hanging on to what it has, with little thought of making more of it. In the church, the energies are spent in "feeding the flock," serving the present members, working to keep the young people in the church. There is little time spent on making new converts.

The *fourth* stage is the point at which the energies of the group are turned inward, with members fighting among themselves to divide the spoils. By this time they have forgotten what it was like to be out there on the cutting edge, scraping to create and build from nothing. They assume that the "goodies" will always be there, that the money will always keep rolling in, and everyone fights for a bigger slice of the pie! There is arguing, squabbling, petty fusses, everyone working to justify his own importance, trying to get ahead of the next guy within the group. So the group stagnates. There is no atmosphere of excitement and mission. Nobody is making a new product, or bringing in new people. Growth stops. And as the pie shrinks, there is less for everyone, and so the fight becomes more rancorous. The downward momentum accelerates.

What is the answer to this downward spiral? *Go back to stage one!* When a group gets its eyes back on the original purpose of the organization, turns its attention back to creating new business or bringing in new people, the spiral can be reversed. The pastor gets out of his study and starts working directly to win new people; the officers of the company lay down their organizational charts to pour their energies into the sales effort of the business; things begin to happen! The growth graphs turn upwards again! When you go back to stage one, good things always begin to happen!

I guess that is why I like the Apostle Paul so much: he never got out of stage one! He never forgot what his job was, what the top priority was. He was a tiger! Once he got on the track, he never was distracted or slowed down. He was a mover, an action guy. He was thrown in jail, so he preached the Gospel to the jailer (*see* Acts 16). He was nearly drowned in a shipwreck and hit the beach preaching the Gospel (*see* Acts 27). He sat in a cell facing the chopping block and wrote letters talking about Jesus (*see* 2 Timothy). He had one speed—full steam; one direction—straight ahead; and only one priority—stage one!

What could happen would be fantastic if the church could get back to that kind of single-mindedness about its role in the world. If we could turn back to that basic goal of bringing new people into the Kingdom and into the church, all the other things—raising the budget, educating the people, helping the poor—would flow naturally from the enormous surge of vitality that would be triggered by all those new, excited Christians in the church. It never fails. When a congregation has become sidetracked by all the nitty-gritty routines of playing church, nothing jolts it back into the mainstream of evangelistic action like influx of new, enthusiastic Christians who have come into the Kingdom too recently to be jaded and ho-hum. The excitement of new converts inspires and motivates the old ones, and forces them to reassess their own commitment. The sleepy Christians are jolted into getting on with the Lord's work, and the momentum builds. But to start the ball rolling, there must be that flood of new believers, and that comes only when the church presses forward with its job of spreading the Gospel to those who do not yet know Jesus Christ as their personal Saviour.

Lord, make me a stage-one man!

Believe!

...in the Family

Introduction

I was blessed with the world's best Mom and Dad.

Mom was filled with love and driven by values. She set the tone for us on faith and virtue and simple kindness toward others. As for Dad, he was a rock. While he traveled a lot, he gave us every ounce of his attention when he was home. He was firm when he needed to be firm and supportive when we needed support. None of us would be who we are without Mom and Dad.

So it deeply concerns me that so many kids don't have a similar family experience as I had. Today, about 40 percent of children are born into a single-parent household. In almost every case, that means the mom. The dad often isn't involved.

Bigger picture, the family itself is in danger. About half of marriages now end in divorce. And looking to the future, nearly 50 percent of adults don't want a family at all.

To be clear, not everyone can get married or have kids, and some marriages need to end. Thank God we don't live in the era when abuse was tolerated or swept under the rug. We don't want to return to those days.

But it's also true that America can't move forward without strong families. If families and marriages falter, more and more children will grow up without the most important relationships that help them get a strong start in life.

...in the Family

The family is the building block of our society, the essential foundation for success. The family is where we find the love that makes us look outside of ourselves. The family is where we find the greatest spur to push ourselves, driven by a desire to provide, protect, nurture, and grow. And the family is where we pass on the values that enable children to lead good, happy, and fulfilling lives.

Children who don't experience a family's love are at much greater risk for everything from bad grades to worse jobs to being in the criminal justice system. In a failing effort to ward off that future, some increasingly farm out the responsibility of raising children to others, including schools and the state. But nothing can replace parents! Children need strong families, and strong families are built around the hopes and opportunities of the rising generation.

As a country, and most importantly as individual Americans, we have to renew the family—fast.

Today's family may look different than it did in decades past, but regardless, we know that a caring family environment remains critical for a child's future success.

Scholar Ian Rowe has spoken often about what he calls the "success sequence." It's a simple process to teach a young person: finish high school, get a job, get married, have children, in that order. Those who follow that sequence have a dramatically more successful future than those who don't.

I'm guessing many parents have taught this to their children, even if they didn't give Ian the credit. I can also imagine that for others, it may be difficult to teach this if it wasn't their personal experience. I trust that adults continue to want the best for the next generation. Sharing excellent advice and empowering a child with wisdom is always worth the effort.

Lord knows, family takes a lot of work. I can attest to that. Maria and I have four headstrong kids. But I can also attest that family is uniquely rewarding. The joys, the challenges, even the sorrows—they have made life far greater than I imagined.

Believe!

What would it take for everyone to find that meaning and fulfillment? Intentionality. Humility. Self-sacrifice. We need to be the best husbands, the best wives, the best fathers, the best mothers we possibly can. Our children, and our country, are counting on it—on us.

—*Doug DeVos*

WHEN WE SPEAK OF THE SURVIVAL of the American way of life, the concept conjures up visions of legislative assemblies, military arsenals, and the pomp and circumstance of governmental ceremony. In fact, the vitality of our American system depends not so much on any of these as it depends on what occurs in the living rooms, dining rooms, dens, and backyards of millions of ordinary, modest, American homes.

It would be difficult to arrange a hierarchy of the institutions which are most vital to our way of life. But it is safe to say that at the head of such a list would come the family. All other institutions—school, economic system, government, even the church—have their basis in the strength of the home and the family. Some sociologists have suggested that the family as we have traditionally known it will be extinct by the end of this century, gone the way of the dinosaur and the dodo bird. I don't believe that. I believe the family is so fundamental to human life that it will never be replaced by any other system. Still, one must admit that an increasingly complex culture has placed great stress on the family, that it no longer occupies the place of sanctity that it once had in the minds of many people.

It is time in America for the family concept to be reaffirmed, time for us to be prodded back to our basic responsibilities as parents, time for us to believe in the family so strongly that we will be willing to make whatever rearrangements of priorities are necessary to make our own homes the incubators of the American dream.

My grandparents came to this country from Holland and settled in western Michigan. I have warm memories of family life going back to earliest childhood. We were close to one another. We struggled sometimes, but we struggled together, and there was always plenty of love that never even had to be expressed in so many words. It was there, and as a child I always could sense it. I came by my interest in salesmanship honestly; my grandfather was an old-fashioned "huckster." He went to the farmer's market every day in an old truck, bought vegetables, and sold them in the community. I was with him the first time I ever sold anything, selling extra onions that he had left over after traveling his regular route.

My dad was an electrician and sold electrical supplies, so the tradition of selling was firmly imbedded in my family life. Dad was a wonderful man. He was as honest as any man who ever lived, and he worked hard all his life. He was frustrated by the fact that he never owned his own business, and his advice to become an independent businessman was one of the important motivating influences on me as a young man. He lived to see me achieve a certain degree of success; Amway had just started rolling when he died in 1962. I believe that before Dad died he had a feeling that Amway would become the success that it has. He told me that the foundation of the company had been honesty and fairness in our dealings; that the people of the company had come to count on Amway and what it stood for, and that I should not let them down. I have never forgotten that.

The point of such reminiscence is the impact of the home in shaping lives. I can look back and see clearly how important my family was to my development. My attitude toward selling as a profession began on that vegetable truck. My attitude toward God began as we bowed our heads around the dinner table. My belief in the power of the will began as I ran along at my father's heels and heard him talk of the limitless potential of the human effort. The large institutions of our society are made up of people, and those people are more the product of the home than of any other single influence. When I trace my own development in the home, and realize that as the father of four children I am now on the other side of the fence, I am sobered and sometimes a bit frightened by the enormity of the responsibility.

That responsibility is a joint one, with the burden falling equally on the father and the mother. But if one of the two fails to take the responsibility seriously, the father is more often than not the culprit. A man, given the task of putting bread on the table, seems to drift away from the demands of the home more easily than the woman.

There is an old adage that says, "If you're too busy to spend time with your family, you're too busy." I believe that. There are some tasks that cannot be delegated and parenthood is one of them. There is no substitute for time spent in the home—quality time, when the members of the family are genuinely accessible to one another. At Amway we work hard to get our men home on weekends. Our conventions never overlap a Sunday. We are sometimes asked, "How can you let your feelings about family life keep you from making that extra profit?" That is no problem with us. We have a simple philosophy: if the money must be made at the expense of the family, we don't need it. It is just not worth it.

I am away from home a lot, but when I am there, I try to let my time be open to the children, to have the time to do the things they want to do. One of the best fathers I know is our chief pilot. He is gone frequently, but when he is home, he is *really* at home. He doesn't sit up and watch television all night; he is accessible to his children. The demands of businesses and careers often are blamed for wrecking homes when the job is not the true cause of the problem. Very few jobs require so much time and energy that a man cannot do them well and still have time for his family. It is not usually the business that wrecks the home; it is the constant Saturdays and Sundays on the golf course, the time spent at the bar on the way home each evening, the nights out with the boys, and a variety of similar routines. The demands of the job become an "out," an excuse to neglect a marriage that is already failing or a homelife that is unpleasant.

Just being present in the home is only the beginning. The decisions to be made, the fine lines to be drawn between proper and improper use of discipline, are difficult and endless. In our family the style of discipline has changed considerably since the earlier days. We went through the whole child-rearing routine of trying to let the children make their own decisions and reach appropriate choices on their own. That sounds good in the child-rearing books, but in our home it didn't work out so well, and as a consequence my own style has become more authoritarian. Certain rules are set and they are inarguable. The children are told, "These are the rules, and you are going to live with them. You can either live with them happily or you can bellyache about them and make us all miserable. But you *are* going to obey them." The trick, of course, is to decide which matters are important enough to warrant that kind of authoritarian approach and which are not.

No family is going to have smooth sailing all the time. If there is going to be a fight in my house over family discipline—and sometimes that is unavoidable—I insist on picking the battleground on which it will be fought. There are many things which irritate me, things which I would prefer to see my children do differently, but some of them are not worth making an issue of. I don't believe that a few inches of hair over a boy's collar is worth a major family hassle. I consider the kind of clothes my children wear an inappropriate battlefield on which to fight the war of adolescent rebellion. If I have to put my foot down, I want to do it on something that is really worth it!

Amway has always placed great emphasis on the family as a unit. We do not recruit men alone or women alone to sell our products when we can recruit the entire family. From the very first, our business has been something that husbands and wives—and even children—could do together. Jay Van Andel and I didn't sit down and say in the beginning, "This is going to be a family business." It just worked out that way. We saw that both the husband and the wife must be convinced before either would do well, so we decided to try to recruit them together. Gradually the family concept evolved, and now it is an important part of the Amway tradition.

At Amway we believe in the family enough to attempt to make involvement in our business something which strengthens family ties rather than threatening them. When we bring our distributors to Grand Rapids for sales seminars, we always bring husband and wife together. We give trips and cruises as incentive prizes, and the couple is always invited.

Even our conventions are family-oriented. When we had one of our first big conventions, the hotel where we held it doubled up on bartenders. Big convention here, they figured, so we'll sell lots of booze this weekend. They expected the bars to be humming. But on the first day the bars stayed empty all day. They couldn't believe it. And so the second day they pulled the extra bartenders off duty and doubled up the waitresses in the coffee shop. Why? Because the Amway crowd wasn't a bunch of guys away from home alone with nothing better to do than to stand around in a bar. It was families doing things together, sharing with each other, and that made for a whole different convention atmosphere.

I don't know the answers to the many questions about child rearing; I'm not sure anyone does. I don't know why some kids seem to absorb the values of their parents more than other kids do; I'll leave that one for the psychologists to worry about. I don't have any advice for young parents about how to run a family; I'm no authority on that. I just do the best I can to be a good father from day to day, and—like everyone else—I'll have to wait a few years to see how things turn out.

But on one point I am willing to be more emphatic: without strong families in America none of the values which we love and live for will survive—or, for that matter, will be worth preserving. Strong families are not made without strong people who believe enough in the value of their parenthood that they are willing to arrange their entire lives, if necessary, around home and family.

How to Practice
These Principles

Conclusion

Now what?

I get this question every time I talk about these time-tested principles. Most people understand them intuitively. If they don't, they quickly get up to speed because these principles speak to every human heart.

But understanding is only the first step. The next step is applying them in everything you do. Belief has to become behavior. When it does, you can transform your life. You can build a stronger family, lead a better career, and find more success, meaning, and fulfillment than ever before—all while lifting up America itself.

So, how can you turn these principles into daily practices? How can you begin to transform your life—and our country?

Bad news: I don't have the answer.

But good news: You do.

There's no template, no formula, for applying these principles because you're unique. You know your life better than I ever could. You have the best grasp of your own passions and purpose. You see opportunities and obstacles that I don't because you're closer to them. And you can apply these principles to seize those opportunities and overcome those obstacles. In fact, you can do it in ways that no one else can.

How to Practice These Principles

While I can't give you an exact roadmap, I can give you some quick directions.

First up: Engage in constant self-reflection. Ask yourself, every day, if you're living out these principles.

Remember that applying principles isn't a one-time thing. It requires constant adjustment. It also requires the humility to recognize when and where you're falling short—and the honesty to recognize that no matter how well you're doing, you can always do better. Self-reflection is how you develop muscle memory that makes these principles second nature.

Second, relentlessly focus on real life.

Don't just ask yourself if you're practicing "family." Ask if there's a relationship you need to repair, an apology you need to offer, a renewed commitment you need to make. By the same token, don't merely ask if you're practicing "human dignity." Ask yourself whether you're putting people in boxes based on their background instead of acknowledging their individuality. And don't just pay lip service to "accountability"—go out and find people who can actually hold you accountable.

Third, be an entrepreneur.

I mean this in the broadest sense. Entrepreneurship isn't merely about starting a business. (Though if that's your best path, great!) Entrepreneurship is ultimately about how you view the world.

Most people see problems. You should seek solutions to those problems, using these principles to guide your actions. That's entrepreneurship.

Most people are fine with the status quo. You should use these principles to envision and pursue a better world. That's entrepreneurship, too.

More than anything else, entrepreneurship is about asking how you can make a difference—not only in your life but in the lives of others. That's what moves America forward: People like you

113

applying your gifts in principled ways to make your community and our country better.

To be a true entrepreneur, you have to believe. Daily life is going to get you down. You'll inevitably doubt your ability to make a difference. You'll toy with the idea that no, you can't really apply these principles because so much of our society is working against them.

But remember that your actions are a spark—a spark that can ignite a fire in yourself, in others, and in our society. This is the story of America. Seemingly ordinary people making an extraordinary difference, simply by leading principled lives.

Isn't that what we need today? Our country is drifting because people are drifting. And our country will decline if people's belief in time-tested principles further declines and ultimately disappears.

You are the antidote, the solution, the source of hope. You always have been. You're capable of so much more than you know.

My dad ingrained this belief in me and my siblings. But he didn't just instill it in us. In his ninety-two years on earth, Rich DeVos went around the country and the world, delivering a simple message everywhere he went. He told millions of people in no uncertain terms: You can do it!

He believed in people because he believed in these principles. And he believed in these principles because he'd seen them transform his own life and the lives of so many others.

Dad isn't here anymore, but he was right: You can do it. You can lead a life of meaning and success. You can steer our country in a better direction. And no one can do it better than you.

TIMELESS RESOURCES

"Selling America" by Rich DeVos

The Declaration of Independence

"Selling America"
by Rich DeVos

When I think of my dad's beliefs, the book you hold in your hands is one of the first things that comes to mind. So does this speech, which my dad first delivered in the 1960s and continually improved over the following two decades. It's an unabashed tribute to the American free enterprise system—and it reminds Americans that we all have a responsibility to encourage each other, to seize opportunity, and to "sell America." I think you'll enjoy it as much as I do.

—Doug DeVos

Believe!

"Selling America" is Rich DeVos's testament to free enterprise. The president of Amway Corporation has won honors, awards, and national acclaim over the years for this and other talks. This particular presentation of "Selling America" was given to 1,800 young people at the National Junior Achievers Conference, when Amway was only seven years old. Since then, the world of Amway has grown to include one million distributors worldwide, and corporate revenues are over $1 billion annually. Many years have passed since this talk was first delivered, but its principles of free enterprise remain as timely as ever. Here is Rich DeVos, "Selling America."

RICH DEVOS:
Fellow Achievers and fellow Americans, Canadian friends from the north, it's an honor to be with you tonight to share a few thoughts about the great system that makes both of these countries the most prosperous on Earth. Before, however, I build you up too much, because you see, you are the tops in Junior Achievement, you're here because of what you've done, you're proven achievers and performers, I would like to give you a little quiz. It goes like this: What I want to know is, before you go out to rebuild the world, have you learned how to clean up your bedroom? Is that a bad question? I don't know.

We live in an age where the Junior Achievement organization and those of you who are gathered here stand contrary to what many people in this country believe. And as I wander, and as you wander, you find people who don't believe that people should be rewarded in direct proportion to the effort they put forth. They think that all people should be treated equally, like in the socialist or the communist government. And that means that everybody should be equal. What they really mean to say is that everybody should be equally poor because that's about where they stand.

But something happens in the minds of people, those who are not here, those who are roaming the streets tonight saying that

118

"Selling America" by Rich DeVos

America and the free enterprise system shared in this country and Canada is not available to them. They claim the American dream passed them by. But something happened in their attitude that they were never exposed to find out how great this system really is.

And, so, it is exciting to be here. I have a couple of little one-liners, we call them, from people who have applied for welfare. And you've got to understand something of their attitude. So here's a gal, and she writes to the welfare department, and she's writing for her neighbor. She says, "Mrs. Jones has not had any clothes for a year and has been visited regularly by the clergy." Now, the next lady writes, she says, "I cannot get sick pay. I have six children. Can you tell why?" And the next lady says, "This is my eighth child. What are you going to do about it?" Now, here's a state of mind which says, "What are you going to do about my problem? What are you going to do to help me?" Implying here that there's nothing she can do to help herself. And another lady says, "Unless I get my husband's money, pretty soon I will be forced to lead an immoral life." And apparently that's her only out. Another one says, "You have changed my little boy to a girl. Will this make a difference?" I hope so. I really do.

Now this is an attitude, isn't it, on the part of people blaming somebody else for their plight? I appreciate the efforts of government to solve people's poverty problem, but I cannot tolerate their constant complaint that it's somebody else's problem that put them there. I believe enough in our system that I maintain anybody who wants to and is willing to put forth the effort can solve their own poverty problem. I think being poor is something many people do. It sort of has to do with being poor by choice. But you see, that doesn't solve the problem, does it? Because somebody, somewhere, has got to reach that person or those persons, millions of them, because they don't know. They don't realize that it can change their life if they'll look at the opportunity in a new perspective.

But you see, the thing we project, the attitude we show, has as much to do with it as anything. So, I want to talk to you about selling

Believe!

America, and I include the Canadians, because I maintain you are Americans because we all live on the North American continent and we share a common system. I, of course, welcome you and I recognize you're Canadians and that we've taken words and say, "We're Americans and you're Canadians." But we all work under the same concept, and that's why the border goes unguarded, and that's why we go back and forth so freely, because we have so much in common.

But when I ask you to sell America, I maintain it's a part of a greater job. I want you to go out from this place to be successful. I want you to achieve. I want you to use the talents God has given, so you can make a contribution. I want you to assume roles of leadership, so you can take those people who don't know that the opportunities are available to them and make them see the light. And maybe all they're waiting for is a word from you. And sometimes that word is so simple. It goes like this, "Hey, John, you can do it." Maybe nobody's ever told him that. You better think about that. My dad used to say that to me. I used to say, "Oh, I can't do this. I can't do that." And he'd say, "You say *can't* once more, and I'll knock your block right through that wall."

So, somebody kept saying to me, as somebody has said to you, "You can do it. You can do it. It does pay. You can get ahead." But you see, those people never had it. Let me give you an example. In your school right now is some girl or some boy who doesn't dress quite as well as you think he ought to. But you've got your own little clique going over there in the corner, haven't you? So, this poor soul who maybe is dressing as best they can walks by, and somebody says, "Look at that." You don't have to say any more than that. They feel a little bad anyway that they can't afford something better. But you see, in that moment, you help to destroy that person. Because you see, that little snicker might just have been the whole thing that broke that girl's heart or that boy's heart. But a friendly word from you could have changed that whole situation.

"Selling America" by Rich DeVos

Some of you are decrying the fact that some kids in your school haven't gone on and they're dropping out and you haven't stopped to wonder about the effect you had on the reason they dropped out. See, you're the bright ones. You're the leaders. You can afford some slop. So you skipped a day. But the problem was, when you skipped, you didn't do it alone. You said, "Come on, John. Go with us for a day. We're going to this lake to go swimming. Oh, we'll skip today." Well, when you came back, it was all right. You caught up in a hurry. So you took a grade down that day; it was all right. It didn't matter to you.

But you know, to John, it might've just knocked the edge off it. Then he slipped just a little behind that day and he never quite caught up. And when the end of the semester came, he flunked the course. Not because he wasn't the greatest, because he wasn't that smart, but he was making it until you taught him a habit or took him away. He couldn't afford that day. You could, but you undermined his whole future because you taught him a bad habit that day.

You see, the little things you do, folks, affect the lives of people every day. There's no escaping the impact you have on others. And certainly, as the leaders in your community, you're just not one of the gang. You're one they point to, they look to, and every word of encouragement can change the lives of the others with whom you live. I gave a talk one day in a high school and I talked about smoking. I'd made some comments about the fact that it's an interesting thing that when you're your age, it's real big shot stuff to smoke. And when you're my age, you're a big shot if you can quit. Now, that's an interesting thing. But I made some implications that I didn't approve of smoking. One young gal came up to me afterwards and she says, "I'll have you know, I smoke." I says, "You're kidding." She was a high schooler. She says, "No, I do." I said, "I don't believe you." She says, "Really, I smoke." "No," I said, "you don't smoke, honey. The cigarette smokes. You're just the sucker. You got to remember that."

121

Believe!

I mentioned the fact that you're the leader, you're the comer, you're the goer, you're the achiever. And as such, others will follow you. But as you progress, and as you assume your roles of leadership and as you excel, I want you to remember something: One of the greatest problems we've got in America today, outside of the racial strife that's going on and we all deplore, is the equal respect for each other. One of the things any minority group is seeking is, "Just respect me for what I am. Don't give me any favors. I'm not asking for that." Most of them aren't asking for that. They're just asking for equal respect and equal opportunity, and it's all of us that are going to change that. That won't happen by accident.

I see it happening between groups of people, between classes of people, as well as groups and racial groups. And so the man said, "Well, I went to college." Well, that's all right. I hope you all go to college. I hope you all graduate. But you know, about half the kids coming out of school aren't going to go to college. And although you may have a greater responsibility because you have greater talent, as a man or a woman, you're not necessarily better than the one who didn't. I want you to remember that. I want you to remember that the next time that fellow comes by who picks up the garbage at your house. He's a fellow American who's using his talent to do what he can do. He, too, is a part of the great mainstream of American life.

I had an interesting experience because I like garbagemen. You wouldn't believe that, but I went up for four weeks in a row—this fellow comes by at six-thirty in the morning—because I wanted to meet him. I said, "Hi, how are you this morning? Just came out to tell you, I appreciate your coming." He looked at me and he says, "Are you just getting up or are you just coming in?" He wasn't sure. I said, "No, really, I just came out to say 'Hello.'" I said, "I appreciate you coming by." Now, if you don't think you appreciate his coming by, you just let him skip you a couple of times, and you'll find out how important he is in your life. About the fourth time I went out there, I said, "I'm just coming out to say 'Hello' again." I said, "I really mean it. I appreciate your coming. Do you realize how important the work is that you do, what it does for the sanitation of this community, how it protects the health and welfare of all the people?" He says, "Well, I'll be damned."

Now, I don't like to use that language, but I portrayed to you his attitude. He said, "I've been picking up garbage for years, man. Nobody ever told me that." And I say to you, isn't it too bad that a fellow American, who's doing what he's able to do, has had no one tell him how important his work is? He says, "You know," he says, "you're one in a million." Well, I don't want to be one in a million. And I ask you, as you go on to positions of leadership, to join me in a crusade of respectability for all your fellow Americans. And I hope you go on to college and get a PhD or whatever it is you're seeking. But I hope you'll always remember that that doesn't make you better than the next guy. It gives you greater responsibility.

I marvel at the PhD who works for us, and he's a wonderful man. I look at the chemists we have, and I notice how helpless they are when it comes to emptying the waste basket. And then I look at the people who come to work and work on the line. And I look at the school bus drivers. We say, "Why, he's just a bus driver." And the other people say, "Well, he's just a businessman. He's just a salesman." Will you eradicate the word *just* from your vocabulary? Nobody is just anything. He's a man or a woman doing what he knows how to do best. That's the real sign. So if a guy fixes your car, remember to greet him. Remember to thank him. If all of us will begin to do this, we can change America. We can break down the barriers between "I'm better than you." There's too much of it. So let's join me in the crusade. Let's remember that the little things make a difference.

There was a time I went in a gas station. Young chap comes up to me. He says, "How do you feel?" I said, "I feel wonderful." He says, "You look sick." I said, "Well, I never felt better in my life." And he said, "Well, I don't know. Your color's bad. You look yellow." Well, I got up, I walked out, went down the street in my car, drove a block, stopped to look at my rear-view mirror to see how I felt. I wasn't so sure. When I got home, I checked both bathrooms, fluorescent lights, regular lights, looked in the mirror. I said, "I think my color's all right." Next morning, I'm still peering in my eyeballs. I wonder if I got yellow jaundice, if my liver's quit. Suddenly, not too sure. I thought I looked all right but still felt a little funny. Got back to that gas station that day, discovered something. They'd just painted the place, a sick, yellow color. Anybody in there looked sick. But you see, somebody who I didn't even know, who wasn't skilled in the arts of medicine or anything else, makes an observation. For twenty-four hours, I'm flipped. And any of you girls wears a new dress to school next fall when you go back to school, and nobody says anything, you're flipped just because nobody's said anything. You might've seen five hundred kids that day, but if only two or three, say, "Hey, that's a good-looking dress," then all of a sudden you wear it proudly.

I had a sport coat like that. I bought it, nobody said "Boo." I began to think it was an ugly thing. One day, I met one gal. She said, "Hey, that's a good-looking sport coat." You know what I said every time I put my sport coat on after that? "Hey, that's a good-looking coat, man." All because one person told me so, and that's how you can change the lives of people. And that's why I wasn't kidding you when I said those few words to your friends and school and elsewhere, of "You can do it," can change their whole life, from a kid who was about to quit, from somebody who's struggling and trying to get along. You see, you're the epitome of respectability. He looks to you. You're on the upper side of the class. So when you say it to him, it's a helping hand going down to lift him up, and you can change his life and revolutionize him.

I'm concerned when I see people in union organizations get up and say, "Why, management, that rotten bunch. They're taking all the money and we're doing all the work. And the salesman he rides around on the company expense account, boy, living off the fat of the land. We do all the work and those salesmen are getting all the money. And the stockholder, why he's the worst of all. He gets paid and he doesn't even punch in." What you see in that are the seeds of destruction. Just as surely when management says, "You can't trust the people in the back end anymore. You let them get away with this, and they'll do the rest. You let them come in five minutes late today, and they'll be ten minutes late tomorrow." I want you to remember that that's not a true statement. And the next time somebody tells it to you, you stand up and challenge him and say, "I don't believe it," because that's not the way it is.

I marvel when I look at the school bus drivers. You're riding with them every morning across America and across Canada. They get in their cars and their buses and they drive and they pick you up and they haul you to school and they take you home, whether it's raining or snowing, no matter what it's doing. You can say, "Well, he's just the bus driver." No, he's not just a bus driver. He's a typical American who can be depended upon, who's trustworthy, who's honest, and who carries out his responsibilities. That's the true American that I know.

Well, the other day you were a little concerned about that policeman. Remember the one who shined his light in your car when you were parking? Remember that one? That's the same one that you yelled for when you heard some noise in the backyard two nights later. And then you couldn't wait to see that light from that same policeman, because he was there to help you again. You never know what they'll get you out of, I'll tell you that.

You know last time you sat around you got to kibitzing a little bit, and you said, "Why that cop stopped me only doing thirty in a twenty-five-mile-an-hour zone." And somebody says, "Yeah, I had the same experience." And somebody else says, "Do you realize what he did to me?" And all I want to do is hear one of you say, "Yes, he stopped us from committing murder. He stopped us from more lawlessness. That's what he did." Because you see, every time you sit around in a bull session and somebody condemns the policeman, and somebody else says, "Yeah, he stopped me, too," all you do is begin to undermine the basic forces of this country. You just keep eroding away at them. You just keep undermining the system, don't you? Because you join in the old pastime of running down groups of people.

To the adults, I always talk to them about PTAs. You know you sit in the PTA meeting, somebody says, "Why, do you know that that teacher hit my little Johnny on the knuckles with a ruler?" I say, "Well, if I know the teacher and I know your Johnny, she should've hit him over the head with a baseball bat."

How many of you took a little time after school was out this year to write a note to your teacher and thank him? Well, if you knew how to spell anyway, that might have been a problem. Didn't think of it, did you? You should have. They spent a lot of time working with you. They never once turned you down when you asked for a little extra help. No, they didn't, not if you really wanted it. But you see, this is what built this country. Labor didn't build it. Management didn't build it. Republicans didn't build it. The Democrats didn't build it. No, all the people built it, each one respecting the other one and giving them their day in court and offering them their praise and saying, "Thanks for the help you gave me," whether it was to the garbageman, the teacher, or the policemen. And together, we built it.

This is a great building we're in. Some architect designed it. Some engineer put some work into it. And they should have their credits, but somebody else got down there in a hole and laid those foundations. Somebody else poured that concrete one bucketful at a time. Somebody else put those fixtures in one fixture at a time. And this is the structure that built our country. And you and I, every time we fail to recognize the part other people play in making it what it is, help to undermine it.

They tell me the American people and our free enterprise system— and this is what you're going to hear, especially the fact that you're a Junior Achiever—they say, "Why, this is a rotten society today, folks." Did you know that? "That dog-eat-dog free enterprise system, why, that's out of date. This is the age of socialism. This is a new age, where we're concerned for our fellow man. This dog-eat-dog, trying to outdo the other guy and make a better product and outsell him, that's not anymore." That's what millions are saying in this country, aren't they?

But you see, what disproves all that is that despite this so-called selfish attitude we're supposed to have, last year the American people reached in their pockets and gave $10 billion away to help somebody else. Through the United Community Funds, or whatever else they happen to believe in, to support it and to their churches. And I never heard anybody yet complain, if it really helped somebody else to see a new day, if it helped somebody else make some progress. No, you see, the average American that I know is concerned for the welfare of his fellow Americans, and he works towards that end and he gives to the causes that will help them. So the next time somebody tells you our system is not conscious of the welfare of others, then you remind them that it's more conscious of it than any other group of people on Earth. I don't find any Red Cross or United Community Fund campaigns going on behind the Iron Curtain these days. I don't see them enjoying the things we have. And neither do you.

Don't tell me our system's out of date. It was never more in date. When they talked to you about the great things of this land, I couldn't help but think. The other night when I was in Los Angeles waiting for a flight back to Chicago, I watched people coming in and going. They're coming in from Hawaii. I like to watch the flights from Hawaii because those are always champagne flights, and the people sort of roll in off the ramp when they come in all off those deals. But you know there wasn't a policeman around saying, "Hey Mac, where are you going?" "I'm going to Honolulu." "Well," he says, "Who says you can go?" He says, "I say I can go." That's all you have to have. "I said I wanted to go," and so you go. It's not that way in most parts of the world.

Believe!

They talk a great deal about when the first jet started to travel, you know what the problem was? They were worried about filling all the seats. And you know the problem is today? They can't get the airplanes in the air fast enough. All the plane manufacturers are two years behind. A couple of our pilots were talking the other day about executive aircraft, and they were telling me that if we wanted to buy a new jet airplane today, it would take us two years before we could get delivery on the models that we're seeking. This is the rewards of our system.

Look at the highways. Look at the factories. People told us, you could never start a business of your own, but we started one in our basement. I don't want to give a commercial, but you see, there are people who ride by our plant in Ada, Michigan, every day. You know what they say? "You can't start a business anymore, today. Why, you know the red tape and the government interference and all the problems of labor and management, you just can't do it." Well, we did it and we sold free enterprise. It's in our name, and we built it in because we believed then, and we believe more so now, that the average person in this country would far rather put forth some extra effort to get ahead than to sit home and wait for somebody from the government to hand them a handout. And we've proven it. [SUSTAINED APPLAUSE]

I thank you, but with all that, I've lost my place. I'll start over, and then we can pick the threads out from there. You see, it's not what we've done. But we believed in people and all they've said is, "Give me a chance to get ahead, and I'll do it." So, for those people who you will meet and who will be telling you that opportunity doesn't exist, I want you to stand up and say, "I don't believe it," because I happen to know that opportunity is greater today in this country than ever. And believe me, friends, there's more opportunity in business than any or all of you will ever be able to take advantage of.

The challenges in the industry are great. I keep reading about the fact that the kids in college today go into the social fields. They want to work for the welfare of others. Well, if you've got any guts, you'll get in business because we provide more welfare than anybody else. We provide employment for seventy-two million people, that's what we do. You see, all these people who are talking about trying to help somebody else are only doing it because they don't have the guts to face the real challenge, which is taking on somebody else. So they run around playing patty cake. They say, "Well, I'll hold your hand. I'll help you." Help you, nothing. Give him a job. That's what'll help him the most.

I like people to go to college, and I've got a couple of friends who go. I'm all for it, but I get tired of these boys and their two-bit theories sitting over there always telling me how important it is to help people, and telling these kids, it's all just the love of somebody else. Well, you better love them or you won't help them. But I'll tell you, you can help a lot more people our way than you can their way. You talk about saying a simple thing with an idea. You say, "I'll tell you what, lady. I'm going to bring the soap to you instead of making you go to the store and get it." And that's all we did. And that's the great thing of our two countries, that it allows people to still apply such technique. And that's why we have the greatest standard of living the world has ever known.

Let me give you a few comparisons between Russia and the United States, because I hear more and more people tell me that our way is out of date. It's an interesting thing. If we're going to enjoy what they have in Soviet Russia, you know what we're going to have to do? If we're going to enjoy what they have, the first thing we're going to have to do is abandon three-fifths of our steel capacity and two-thirds of our petroleum output. Then, we'll have to get rid of 95 percent of our electric motor capacity. And then, we've got to destroy two of every three of our hydroelectric plants and we'll get along on a tenth of our present volume of natural gas. Then, we'll rip up fourteen of every fifteen miles of our paved highways and two of every three miles of our railroad tracks. Then we'll sink eight of every nine oceangoing ships that we have and we'll scrap nine-teen out of every twenty automobiles and trucks. Now, you know the problem don't you? You see, what bothers the people in Russia is that they've got all the parking places and we've got all the automobiles. Now, that's a real problem there.

Now, the next thing we're going to do is we're going to cut our living standard by three fourths. We're going to destroy forty million television sets, nine …[AUDIENCE INTERRUPTION] Wouldn't that be wonderful? That reminds me, nine out of every ten tele-phones. Some of you are going to have to learn to write and spell again, and that gets pretty tough, you see? After we got rid of nine out of every ten telephones, we're going to get rid of seven out of every ten houses. Yeah, and some of you would discover that you can't spend so much time in the bathroom. Now, I tell you, one john down at the end of the hall shared with seven families. You see, we sit and we laugh, and they tell me our system isn't worth preserv-ing. Isn't it marvelous, that wall they built around Berlin to keep all of us out? Did you ever notice that we don't have any "out-igra-tion" quota in this country? Yeah. Anybody is free to leave, but they don't want to.

Well, after we get rid of those houses and telephones, then, to keep up with them, we'll put sixty million people back on the farm—on the farm to try and grow enough food. Most of you wouldn't be wondering about what you're going to do when you get out of school. That would have already been predetermined by the gov-ernment. And most of you would already be back on the farm, and they still can't raise enough food to feed their own people. And yet I read about these boys, and they're telling me that that system's a wonderful one. And somebody says, "Your theories are all wrong." And all I can say to the boys with the theories is, "Friend, I'm not talking theory."

I had the privilege of having dinner this evening with Mr. Moseler and Mr. Hardenbrook. And Mr. Moseler was telling me some boys in college challenge him and say, "Mr. Moseler, you're out of date. What you're telling me is theory." Mr. Moseler said, "I'm not telling you a theory, friend. I'm telling you performance figures from a businessman. Those boys who are writing those books over in college, they got the theory. I got the facts, and what I've been giving you is facts."

The United States of America, and I don't have the figures on Canada or I'd share them, but they apply equally because we've checked the map and the performance of the Canadian people is just the same as it is here, but the figures for this country show that the United States has 6 percent of the world's population. We occupy 7 percent of its land surface. However, we own 71 percent of the world's automobiles, 56 percent of its telephones, 50 percent of the radios, 29 percent of the railroads and 83 percent of all the television sets. You might like to know that the people of the United States own 90 percent of the world's bathtubs, too. This country produces 59 percent of the world's steel, 46 percent of its electric power, 50 percent of the oil, 56 percent of the corn, 42 percent of the cotton, 33 percent of the coal, 31 percent of the copper, 38 percent of the iron, and 44 percent of all the manufactured goods in the world is made by 6 percent ...[APPLAUSE INTERRUPTION] is made by 6 percent of the world's population.

And these boys with their theories are telling you it doesn't work. Well, young friends, it's up to those of us who know better to stand up and challenge those...well, I can't think of a favorable word at the moment. But you see, if we don't challenge them, they'll take the day. I was in a barbershop a while back. A fella came in, he obviously worked on a railroad, sat down, and the first thing he did, he started grumbling. He grumbled about the railroad. He grumbled about his working conditions and said, "Why, it's too bad they make me work overtime. They pay me too much." And they don't do this. And they don't do that. Oh, he went on and on. Oh yeah, they paid him too much because, you see, he didn't want to work that hard. He couldn't stand the overtime. He wanted to go home. And so every-thing was wrong. Finally, he says, "The government ought to take over the railroad."

And about that time, I was going right through the roof. I says, "Friend, I know a place in the world they do it your way. And there's nothing keeping you here. In fact, I got enough money in my pocket to buy you a ticket, one way. And you can go, because you don't have to stay here and do it our way." But he got kind of mad and he left, and I left. But you see, that wasn't the clue. What I'm trying to say to you is this, that every time he comes in the barber shop now, he does it differently. See, before this, always when he came in, he grumbled about how rotten our society was and our system was. But now, they tell me when he comes in, he sits down and he looks around. He's afraid I might be there again.

But the core of this and the problem is that he'd been coming to the barbershop for years, and nobody challenged him. You see, he kept downgrading America every time he came in and he got away with it. And if you say something long enough, pretty soon you begin to believe it. And pretty soon you think everybody believes it. And pretty soon you've dug your own grave only because a few of us didn't stand up and say, "Hey, Mac, it's not that way. Let me tell you about how great it is in America. Let me tell you how great it is to be a Canadian." Until we start to do that, we too will contribute to our own demise.

A fellow by the name of Robert Murphy, a former diplomat, former undersecretary of state, said this, "Only by fostering private enterprise can the United States truly capitalize on its most basic advantage over communism." And another fellow from England by the name of Winston Churchill, said this, "Socialism is a philosophy of failure, the creed of ignorance, and the gospel of envy. Its inherent virtue is the equal sharing of misery."

And I would close with these words: To me, the strength of our system doesn't necessarily lie in the free enterprise system, but it lies in the fact that we have always had mutual respect for each other and we will be no greater than that respect. And at the bottom of that respect lies a faith that most of us believe that we are placed on this earth by God with a responsibility to use the talents we have been given. And certainly, the prayer that we had at the opening of this session said the same, that this is our real responsibility today. When this country was founded and the pilgrims came here, they had a Thanksgiving Day and they gave thanks. And they pioneered and they went forth, and they used their talents. I find today in Washington an effort to get rid of the words "In God We Trust" on our money.

And in my opinion, when they get rid of the words, you better get ready to throw the money away, because it won't be worth anything either. And I happen to believe …[APPLAUSE INTERRUPTION]

Just as surely as I stand up for our system, I stand up for my religious beliefs. And too many people are always backing off, because someplace, somebody said, "Well, don't discuss religion and politics, because all it leads to is an argument." Well, young people, it's time we took on the argument and it's time we debated every issue and it's time (when) everybody else started telling us what's wrong, we stood up and said, "Hey man, let me tell you what's right." And you watch the other crowd. They'll wilt, because they don't have the performance figures to back 'em up. They just got theory.

When somebody tells me our system's out of date, I ask them how many people from the free world were shot climbing into Berlin on the other side. And I ask how many tunnels were dug from this side. And what's happened is that the rest of the world is in one big prison camp, trying to escape to the freedoms that we enjoy. And you and I better shout about it. And whenever anybody will tell you it ain't so, you tell them it is. We believe, and have always believed, in this country, that man was created in the image of God, and that he was given talents and responsibilities, and was instructed to use them, to make this world a better place in which to live. And you see, this is the really great thing of America. And this is where it contrasts with everything that Russia and other godless societies are attempting to do.

Because you see, at heart, we believe that man was created and that in him is a living spirit. That he's not just a bunch of dirt and clay put together for a few years until we bury him, but that he has greater depth and greater responsibilities than that. And that's why we respect each other. That's why we care for each other. And that's why we must stand together and give thanks for the things we enjoy.

And so I'm asking you to sell America, along with whatever business or profession you go into. I want to remind you of your position of responsibility as a leader, because that you are. You've proven it by coming here. But remember to extend that greeting and a friendly hand to all your fellow Americans and your fellow Canadians, because they, too, were created in the image of God. And with your respectability, regardless of where they come from or their color or their economic station, we'll go together as a united people, building a country that can go on and on and on with the blessings of God.

Let me close with these words, and they are taken from Thomas Wolfe. And he said this, "So, then, to every man his chance—to every man, regardless of his birth, his shining golden opportunity—to every man, the right to live, to work, to be himself, and to become whatever thing his manhood and his vision can combine to make him—this, seeker, is the promise of America."

ANNOUNCER:

The Declaration
of Independence

As Americans prepare to celebrate our country's 250th anniversary on July 4, 2026, it's worth remembering what exactly happened on that day. Our founders gave us the Declaration of Independence—a charter of freedom that lays out the principles that have guided our country ever since. Our duty today is to follow in the footsteps of those who came before us, applying these principles to solve society's problems and move forward together. We have a duty to realize the promise of "Life, Liberty, and the Pursuit of Happiness" for all.

—Doug DeVos

In Congress, July 4, 1776

The unanimous Declaration of the thirteen united States of America

When in the Course of human events, it becomes necessary for one people to dissolve the political bands which have connected them with another, and to assume among the powers of the earth, the separate and equal station to which the Laws of Nature and of Nature's God entitle them, a decent respect to the opinions of mankind requires that they should declare the causes which impel them to the separation.

We hold these truths to be self-evident, that all men are created equal, that they are endowed by their Creator with certain unalienable Rights, that among these are Life, Liberty and the pursuit of Happiness—That to secure these rights, Governments are instituted among Men, deriving their just powers from the consent of the governed,—That whenever any Form of Government becomes destructive of these ends, it is the Right of the People to alter or to abolish it, and to institute new Government, laying its foundation on such principles and organizing its powers in such form, as to them shall seem most likely to effect their Safety and Happiness. Prudence, indeed, will dictate that Governments long established should not be changed for light and transient causes; and accordingly all experience hath shewn, that mankind are more disposed to suffer, while evils are sufferable, than to right themselves by abolishing the forms to which they are accustomed. But when a long train of abuses and usurpations, pursuing invariably the same Object evinces a design to reduce them under absolute Despotism, it is their right, it is their duty, to throw off such Government, and to provide new Guards for their future security—Such has been the patient sufferance of these Colonies; and such is now the necessity which constrains them to alter their former Systems of Government. The history of the present King of Great Britain is a history of repeated injuries and usurpations, all having in direct object the establishment of an absolute Tyranny over these States. To prove this, let Facts be submitted to a candid world.

He has refused his Assent to Laws, the most wholesome and necessary for the public good.

He has forbidden his Governors to pass Laws of immediate and pressing importance, unless suspended in their operation till his Assent should be obtained; and when so suspended, he has utterly neglected to attend to them.

He has refused to pass other Laws for the accommodation of large districts of people, unless those people would relinquish the right of Representation in the Legislature, a right inestimable to them and formidable to tyrants only.

He has called together legislative bodies at places unusual, uncomfortable, and distant from the depository of their public Records, for the sole purpose of fatiguing them into compliance with his measures.

He has dissolved Representative Houses repeatedly, for opposing with manly firmness his invasions on the rights of the people.

He has refused for a long time, after such dissolutions, to cause others to be elected; whereby the Legislative powers, incapable of Annihilation, have returned to the People at large for their exercise; the State remaining in the mean time exposed to all the dangers of invasion from without, and convulsions within.

He has endeavoured to prevent the population of these States; for that purpose obstructing the Laws for Naturalization of Foreigners;

refusing to pass others to encourage their migrations hither, and rais-ing the conditions of new Appropriations of Lands.

He has obstructed the Administration of Justice, by refusing his Assent to Laws for establishing Judiciary powers.

He has made Judges dependent on his Will alone, for the tenure of their offices, and the amount and payment of their salaries.

He has erected a multitude of New Offices, and sent hither swarms of Officers to harrass our people, and eat out their substance.

He has kept among us, in times of peace, Standing Armies with-out the Consent of our legislatures.

He has affected to render the Military independent of and supe-rior to the Civil power.

He has combined with others to subject us to a jurisdiction for-eign to our constitution, and unacknowledged by our laws; giving his Assent to their Acts of pretended Legislation:

For Quartering large bodies of armed troops among us:

For protecting them, by a mock Trial, from punishment for any Murders which they should commit on the Inhabitants of these States:

For cutting off our Trade with all parts of the world:

For imposing Taxes on us without our Consent:

For depriving us in many cases, of the benefits of Trial by Jury:

For transporting us beyond Seas to be tried for pretended offences:

For abolishing the free System of English Laws in a neigh-bouring Province, establishing therein an Arbitrary government, and enlarging its Boundaries so as to render it at once an exam-ple and fit instrument for introducing the same absolute rule into these Colonies:

For taking away our Charters, abolishing our most valuable Laws, and altering fundamentally the Forms of our Governments:

For suspending our own Legislatures, and declaring themselves invested with power to legislate for us in all cases whatsoever.

The Declaration of Independence

He has abdicated Government here, by declaring us out of his Protection and waging War against us.

He has plundered our seas, ravaged our Coasts, burnt our towns, and destroyed the lives of our people.

He is at this time transporting large Armies of foreign Mercenaries to compleat the works of death, desolation and tyranny, already begun with circumstances of Cruelty & perfidy scarcely paralleled in the most barbarous ages, and totally unworthy the Head of a civilized nation.

He has constrained our fellow Citizens taken Captive on the high Seas to bear Arms against their Country, to become the executioners of their friends and Brethren, or to fall themselves by their Hands.

He has excited domestic insurrections amongst us, and has endeavoured to bring on the inhabitants of our frontiers, the merciless Indian Savages, whose known rule of warfare, is an undistinguished destruction of all ages, sexes and conditions.

In every stage of these Oppressions We have Petitioned for Redress in the most humble terms: Our repeated Petitions have been answered only by repeated injury. A Prince, whose character is thus marked by every act which may define a Tyrant, is unfit to be the ruler of a free people.

Nor have We been wanting in attentions to our Brittish brethren. We have warned them from time to time of attempts by their legislature to extend an unwarrantable jurisdiction over us. We have reminded them of the circumstances of our emigration and settlement here. We have appealed to their native justice and magnanimity, and we have conjured them by the ties of our common kindred to disavow these usurpations, which, would inevitably interrupt our connections and correspondence. They too have been deaf to the voice of justice and of consanguinity. We must, therefore, acquiesce in the necessity, which denounces our Separation, and hold them, as we hold the rest of mankind, Enemies in War, in Peace Friends.

Believe!

We, therefore, the Representatives of the united States of America, in General Congress, Assembled, appealing to the Supreme Judge of the world for the rectitude of our intentions, do, in the Name, and by Authority of the good People of these Colonies, solemnly publish and declare, That these United Colonies are, and of Right ought to be Free and Independent States; that they are Absolved from all Allegiance to the British Crown, and that all political connection between them and the State of Great Britain, is and ought to be totally dissolved; and that as Free and Independent States, they have full Power to levy War, conclude Peace, contract Alliances, establish Commerce, and to do all other Acts and Things which Independent States may of right do. And for the support of this Declaration, with a firm reliance on the protection of divine Providence, we mutually pledge to each other our Lives, our Fortunes and our sacred Honor.

Georgia
Button Gwinnett
Lyman Hall
George Walton

North Carolina
William Hooper
Joseph Hewes
John Penn

South Carolina
Edward Rutledge
Thomas Heyward, Jr.
Thomas Lynch, Jr.
Arthur Middleton

Massachusetts
John Hancock

Maryland
Samuel Chase
William Paca
Thomas Stone
Charles Carroll of Carrollton

Virginia
George Wythe
Richard Henry Lee
Thomas Jefferson
Benjamin Harrison
Thomas Nelson, Jr.
Francis Lightfoot Lee
Carter Braxton

The Declaration of Independence

Pennsylvania
Robert Morris
Benjamin Rush
Benjamin Franklin
John Morton
George Clymer
James Smith
George Taylor
James Wilson
George Ross

Delaware
Caesar Rodney
George Read
Thomas McKean

New York
William Floyd
Philip Livingston
Francis Lewis
Lewis Morris

New Jersey
Richard Stockton
John Witherspoon
Francis Hopkinson
John Hart
Abraham Clark

New Hampshire
Josiah Bartlett
William Whipple

Massachusetts
Samuel Adams
John Adams
Robert Treat Paine
Elbridge Gerry

Rhode Island
Stephen Hopkins
William Ellery

Connecticut
Roger Sherman
Samuel Huntington
William Williams
Oliver Wolcott

New Hampshire
Matthew Thornton

Join Us at
TheBelieveJournal.com

Bringing entreprenuers, civic leaders, and everyday Americans together to dicuss the principles that both unite us and set us apart from the pack. God, America, and Free Enterprise—this is what the Founding Fathers started with, and this is what we Believe!

About the Authors

Rich DeVos (March 4, 1926 – September 6, 2018) was a visionary entrepreneur, philanthropist, and co-founder of Amway, the world's largest direct selling company. Born in Grand Rapids, Michigan, Rich built a global business with his lifelong friend Jay Van Andel, grounded in the belief that anyone, given the opportunity, could succeed.

A devout Christian, Rich often described himself as "a sinner saved by grace." His faith shaped his values, guiding his approach to business, philanthropy, and Family. He believed deeply in the American dream and the power of free enterprise, personal responsibility, and perseverance.

Rich was a dynamic motivational speaker, known for energizing audiences with his unwavering belief in people's potential. Alongside his beloved wife, Helen, he dedicated himself to strengthening communities both in his hometown and globally. He also brought his passion for leadership and excellence to the world of sports as the owner of the NBA's Orlando Magic.

Above all, Rich cherished his roles as husband, father, grandfather, and great-grandfather. His legacy lives on through his Family, his writings, and the countless lives he touched through his generosity, leadership, and enduring optimism.

Believe!

Doug DeVos is an advocate for opportunity and freedom for all. He is Co-Chair of the Board of Directors for Amway, the world's largest direct-selling company. He served as President of Amway for more than 16 years.

Doug is a global ambassador for entrepreneurship and a devoted philanthropist, locally and nationally. He's Chairman of Stand Together's Frederick Douglass Society, an organization committed to helping people realize their potential by addressing society's biggest challenges. He is also Chairman of the Board for the National Constitution Center in Philadelphia and is involved in numerous Michigan business and civic organizations.

Doug is a passionate sailor and serves as Principal of the American Magic, a professional sailing franchise. He holds a Bachelor of Science Degree from Purdue University's Krannert School of Business and played on the Purdue football team. Doug and his wife, Maria, are active members of the Keystone Community Church. They have four married children and four grandchildren and counting.